HIGHWAY 61

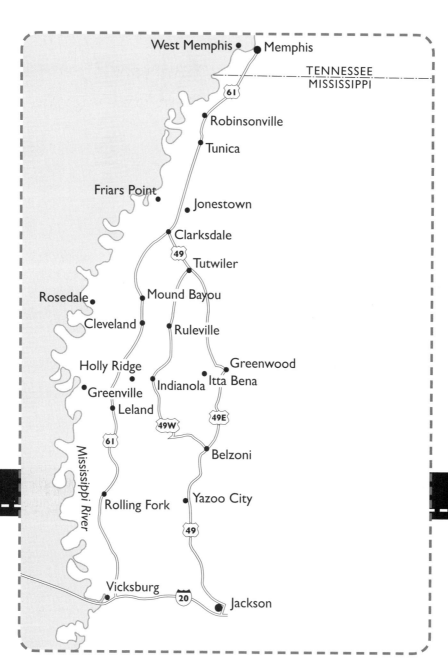

The Mississippi Delta

Edited by Randall Norris

Photographs by Jean-Philippe Cyprès

With a Foreword by Morgan Freeman

HIGHWAY 61

Heart of the Delta

The University of Tennessee Press   Knoxville

Frontispiece: The Mississippi Delta.

Library of Congress Cataloging-in-Publication Data

Highway 61 : heart of the Delta / edited by Randall Norris ; photographs by Jean-Philippe Cyprès ; with a foreword by Morgan Freeman.
  p. cm.
Includes index.
ISBN-13: 978-1-57233-614-8 (hardcover: alk. paper)
ISBN-10: 1-57233-614-5

 1. Delta (Miss. : Region)—Biography—Anecdotes.
 2. Delta (Miss. : Region)—Social conditions—Anecdotes.
 3. Delta (Miss. : Region)—Sociallife and customs—Anecdotes.
 4. Delta (Miss. : Region)—Pictorial works.
 I. Norris, Randall, 1949–
 II. Cyprès, Jean-Philippe, 1959–
 III. Title: Highway sixty-one.

F347.Y3H54 2008
976.2'40630922—dc22
[B]   2007046302

To Linda, the most important woman in my life.

—R. N.

To my family, with deepest love and admiration.

—J.-P.

Contents

PART IV.

Working the Land and Water:
A Photo Essay

PART V.

A Delta Dream

My Mississippi Delta Story

Morgan Freeman

The Mississippi Delta started out as a swampy, mosquito-infested forest prime-val. No one attempted to cut it down until the early 1820s. The Delta was just too wet, but once it was drained, revealing its wealth of alluvial soil, it became one of the most economically viable places in the country, and the best crop that was ever planted here was cotton. The land itself is a big part of our history. Unfortunately, sometimes all you see is our history, and some parts of our history aren't pretty. Some of my ancestors were slaves who worked these fields. They worked cotton from daylight to dark, and I guess that's why my father didn't want to work in the fields. My father was a hustler of the first order. He did whatever he needed to in order for us to survive, and to keep food on the table and him out of the fields. One of the things that he did to improve his income was move to Chicago. And, like so many people who moved to Chicago, he went up north with high hopes. He thought he'd found the Promised Land.

"One of the smartest moves I've made in life was coming back home to the Mississippi Delta."

But then he saw it for what it was—insidious and painful. He wanted to believe he was freer. But he wasn't. So my folks came back home to the Delta, even though the history they had left was still here. I grew up in a segregated society, one that was purposely, obviously, openly segregated. I didn't have any illusions. I graduated from Greenwood High School, one of those separate but equal schools. The facilities might have been second-class, but the teachers were first-rate.

When I was in high school there were still *White* and *Colored* drinking fountains and waiting rooms. And black people couldn't go to movies at the Paramount Theater in Greenwood unless we sat in the balcony, but that's the way life was back then. We sat in the balcony, and the whites sat on the first floor. Some people say that situation should have bothered me, but it can't bother you if that's the way you are raised. If you're raised up in Africa where people eat worms, you'd eat worms, too, and it wouldn't bother you. If you're growing up in a segregated society, you just do the best you can to get by. I wasn't thinking about rising up and going to the Paramount demanding to be let in on the ground floor; I just wanted to go to the movies! But that's the mistake most people make who are from outside the Delta: they think our history was all bad, but it wasn't.

When I was a kid in high school we used to hang out in a little joint in Greenwood that was a jukebox-fed club called The Stand. All of us kids would go there, and on the weekend the whole building would bounce because all the dancers were dancing to the same beat. We had a ball! Our mothers and grandmothers didn't want us hanging out at places like that. Their edict was "If I catch you in there, you're dead." Their experience with jukes was that there was nothing good going on in those places—just people fighting, cussing, drinking, and sometimes getting hurt or killed.

That's why the jukes had another name: they were known as the buckets of blood. "Where you goin' tomorrow night?" a friend might say. And I'd reply, "I'll see you at the bucket of blood." I must confess, even though my mother and my grandmother didn't want me to go, I went anyway. It was wonderful.

When I left here in 1955 and joined the air force, like so many other young kids from Greenwood, my goal in life was just to get out of the Delta. I know a lot of young men from the Delta found equality in the service, but it was just the opposite for me. I had a bunkmate from California who sat down one afternoon and told me all the things he had ever heard about black people. I've never heard such a mess of misconceptions and stereotypes. The last thing he said was "Why, you're even cleaner than I am." That one really stuck with me. He was raised up to think I was some kind of animal. What a terrible thing to do to a kid! That was when I realized it wasn't just people down south that had those kinds of attitudes; people all over the country had them. I thought it was sad.

At that time I didn't think I'd ever come back to the Delta, and it was years later before I changed my mind. I started coming back about 1979 to visit my parents because they had moved back home in the late 1950s. I couldn't understand

why they had come back. I asked them "What in the world would make you come back here?" They just smiled, and it took me about twenty years to figure that one out: this is home. This is where I grew up. This is what I know. It's the Mississippi Delta. It's the food, and the people, and the place, and it's also the music, because Clarksdale is the legendary home of the blues.

The Delta blues actually originated right here. This is where Robert Johnson supposedly sold his soul to the Devil one dark night at a crossroads near Highway 61, and that was the beginning of the modern blues. But the blues really started a hundred or two hundred years ago. When European orchestras were playing Beethoven and Bach in opera houses, a beautiful thing, the blues, was created right here at the same time, in back rooms, under shade trees, beside cotton gins, and in little juke joints all over the Delta.

The jukes were usually just tarpaper shacks sitting out in the middle of a cotton field or on the edge of the woods. But it wasn't where the music was played that was important but what went on inside the buildings. These were places where people were really jammin'! People just fell in there and had a good time, and they didn't worry about the heat, or the work, or the landlord, or anything else. They decorated the place with catch-as-catch-can furniture, oil tablecloths, and chairs that didn't match. They sold beer by the bucket or the quart and whiskey by the pint. For food they usually had fried catfish, and for entertainment people danced and listened to someone playing blues in the front, while they gambled in the back.

When Bill Luckett and I opened our club, Ground Zero, in Clarksdale, we wanted to make it as authentic as possible because this is a historic venue. This is where it all started. We realized that so much was being done to preserve European classical music, but not enough was being done to preserve American classical music. That's why an authentic blues club was so important—because so many people were coming through here looking for the storied Delta blues. But we didn't just jump into it head-first. We looked a long time before we found the right building, and we read several books that documented the history of juke joints throughout the Delta. People were coming to Clarksdale from Scandinavia, from Asia, from Europe, from all over America to see it—to experience it—and we wanted to give them what they were looking for. We wanted them to sample some real southern hospitality and have a good time. Then they could go home and tell their friends about it, and their friends could come down here and visit. Basically, we just wanted them to get a taste of some real southern hospitality, which is one of the reasons I came home.

Madidi
Gourmet Restaurant
Clarksdale

One of the smartest moves I've made in life was coming back home to the Mississippi Delta. When people found out I was moving back they'd say, "Oh my God! Why Mississippi? You could live anyplace in the world you want! Why are you moving to Mississippi?" And I said, "Precisely because I can live anyplace in the world I want." It took me a long time to figure out, but now I understand why my folks were smiling when they moved back here in the 1950s. Whenever I came back home, I always got that same feeling I had as a kid growing up—closeness, comfort, and security. It may sound strange to you, but that's my Mississippi Delta story.

Acknowledgments

A book this long in the making acquires many debts that can never be repaid. Toward that end, however, we would like to thank all of our contributors: Morgan Freeman, Patti Carr Black, Christine Wilson, Nikki Giovanni, David Jordan, Robin Rushing, and all of our informants. We would also like to acknowledge the people and institutional support that were provided by Sid Graves, Delta Blues Museum; Barbara Carpenter, Mississippi Humanities Council; and Tom Wacaster, Phil Hardin Foundation. We would also like to thank Bill Luckett for his invaluable assistance. In addition, thanks to all the people who contributed to this book in both large and small ways, including Tom Rankin, Dr. Patricia Johnson, Dr. and Mrs. Everette Ryan, Mr. and Mrs. Avery Rowland, Dave Rowland, Jack and Connie Chadwell, Lindell Agee, and, most especially, Pat and Cindy Ryan. Finally, we would like to thank Phil Savage for his contribution of photographs, and Scot Danforth, University of Tennessee Press, whose vision and editorial assistance made this book possible. Thank you one and all!

Grandmother and Next Generation
Vicksburg

Introduction

Randall Norris

When I first started traveling the dusty dirt roads of the Mississippi Delta in 1969, I was with two friends, an army buddy, Pat Ryan, son of Dr. Everette Ryan from Charleston, and Pat's friend, Dave Rowland, son of Avery Rowland, whose farm is in Oakland, and whose home sits at the bottom of a hill on Valley Road. I quickly discovered that, in the Delta at the time, whose son you were dictated how highly you were regarded.

We were on leave, just two weeks away from helicopter pre-flight training at Ft. Wolters, Texas. While we waited to participate in a program that guaranteed a tour of duty in a clearly lost war in Vietnam, we spent long, leisurely days traveling around the Delta. We drove from Sammy Bell's Drive-In to the Charleston VFW Club (where we shot pool and stuck quarters in the only slot machine in town). From there we went to the Crossroads and Linlews in Starkville and finally, Pat's soon to be father-in-law's house, in Tutwiler, where highway 49 East and 49 West join.

Wherever we went, our army uniforms and regulation haircuts gave us enough status to get free beers, mixed drinks, oysters, shrimp, and all the barbecued pork and steak dinners we could eat. That's how I was introduced to the Mississippi Delta, with a tour guide whose left hand held the steering wheel of my yellow Mustang Mach I, and whose right hand gently waved in the hot Delta air when he made a point, like a conductor directing an orchestra.

I also saw a darker side of the Delta: the country store at the crossroads in Money, Mississippi, where Emmett Till's apparent misunderstanding of local customs cost him his life. Later, as the sun hung high overhead, I stood on a muddy bank beside the Tallahatchie River, where Till was found, beaten and filled with bullet holes, a gin fan tied around his neck. Finally, my trip ended that day at the courthouse in Sumner, where Till's killers were "tried." Emmett Till's murder has long been recognized as the catalyst that jumpstarted the Civil Rights movement in America, where four hundred years of wrongs were waiting to be righted, and "big" and "little" issues were dealt with, including the daily indignities African Americans in the Delta had been forced to endure during a hundred years of Jim Crow.

In 1969, in courthouse after courthouse, I saw pristine clean restrooms marked by *Whites Only* signs, or, in the middle of many a town square, I saw a filthy, barely working water fountain labeled *Colored*. I saw a fifty-year-old over-seer slapping his hat against his leg, still using the same harsh language with his workers, when a kind word would have done the job better. I saw the curious smiles and hollow-eyed looks from women standing on the falling-down porches of tarpaper shacks. I also watched as a black man or woman stepped off the side-walk when a white man or woman passed, just because it had always been that way. And I could see the difficulty people found in registering to vote, even though that supposedly had all changed.

That fall I saw things up close and personal—I felt the heat, slapped at the mosquitoes, and smelled the sweet, sickly smell of chemicals being sprayed on the cotton and soybean fields. My experience resonated with that of Patricia Johnson, one of the organizers of the Clarksdale Sunflower Blues Festival, who said: "That's one thing I noticed right off when I came to the Delta. It's such a hot, flat place, that things rise up right in front of you, and you have to deal with them, whether you want to or not." I was forced to deal with things I had never seen in East Tennessee. That was the way it was then, in September 1969, when I first entered the Mississippi Delta.

Since then, I have been back, dozens of times, to this place where each trip sometimes seemed like I was traveling to a foreign country. But, unlike others, who could only see the Delta's painful past, I felt, as much as knew, that what I was seeing was different. What was rising up in front of me in the heat from the rich, black swampy dirt was a caterpillar that some day, some way, stood a good chance of changing into an incredibly beautiful butterfly. When that happened, I wanted to be there to see it fly. And I wasn't the only one.

In 1990, I managed to pick up a traveling companion, Jean-Philippe Cyprès, a world-class, award-winning French photographer. J.-P., as he is called by his friends, a veteran of photo shoots around the world, could also sense the changes that were occurring. With a steady hand and a compassionate lens, he documented them all over the Delta.

He caught the smiling doormen and the ducks on their afternoon stroll through the lobby of the Peabody Hotel in Memphis, and he photographed the twenty-story casinos rising high above Tunica, lighting up the night with huge neon signs, and turning what had been a sleepy, third-world town into a thriving city with one of the strongest tax bases in the United States. He also hung outside a sputtering Cessna 150 to get an afternoon shot of the Humphreys County catfish farms, which stretched far into the future. It was evident farms here were no longer locked into the cotton and rice economy, but were now dedicated to aquaculture and corn for ethanol. Decades-old plantations had given way to European conglomerates. And then there were the people.

One weekend, on Early Wright's Sunday Morning Gospel Hour over 1450AM in Clarksdale, J. P.'s camera caught the splendid image of an elderly woman shar-ing her ancient prayer: "Thank you God," she said, "for not letting my laying down bed become my cooling-off board, and for not letting the walls of my room become the walls of my tomb!"

Farther south, at Tutwiler, Aleck Miller, better known as Sonny Boy Williamson II, one of the greatest harmonica players who ever lived, is buried in weed-covered Wrightman Cemetery next to his two sisters, Mary and Julie. His tombstone has become a memorial, and the photograph entitled *Harpman* documents the silent tribute. Visitors and fellow musicians often leave a cherished trinket, such as a photograph or a favorite harmonica. Less than a mile away from Williamson's grave, in downtown Tutwiler, where contemporary mural painter Cristen Craven Barnard paints larger-than-life pastel murals on Tutwiler's crumbling brick buildings, is Railroad Park. It was here, in 1903, that W. C. Handy claimed he first heard a local musician playing *"Yellow Dog Blues"* on an old guitar, using a knife for a slide.

Farther south, at Rosedale, J. P.'s wide-angled lens caught the fast-moving hands of two women making Delta tamales at the local grocery store, while an old man sat on the steps outside with a guitar in his hands, shouting, "Gimme a dollar! Gimme a dollar!" for taking his picture. Even farther south, on Highway 61, we found the old high school at Shaw, where oil-soaked floors and silver radiators remind everyone who sees *Shaw High School Memories* how their school looked in the 1950s and 1960s. Across the street from the high school, Mr. and Mrs. Jang show us pictures of their five children hanging on the wall behind the counter of their grocery store, and proudly tell us that each of them, in turn, became the class valedictorian.

In Greenville we were fortunate enough to get our hair cut by local barber Sandy D'Angelo who is of Italian descent. He filled us in on the migratory patterns of Italians who had moved into the Delta. Inside his barbershop where the photograph *Next!* was shot, he maintains a store in the back room, where only the finest Mediterranean olives, angel hair pasta, pepperoni, and cheese are sold. Just outside his door the local high school football team was doing calisthenics, in full gear, ignoring the boiling temperatures, concentrating instead on the upcoming Friday night game.

From Yazoo City we took US Highway 3 south to Vicksburg, where some of the most dramatic photographs in the book were taken. A two-hour trip one late afternoon through the Vicksburg National Park yielded the smiling *Lawnmower Army,* a dozen maintenance men whose lawnmowers were tied to ropes so they could pull them up and down the steep hills throughout the park. The park also produced the picture *Now and Then,* an important juxtaposition of a twenty-first-century park ranger leaning against a nineteenth-century Yankee smoothbore cannon that had filled no telling how many southern graves beneath the white crosses guarded by Theodore O'Hara's poem "Bivouac of the Dead."

At the back gate of Vicksburg National Park, J. P. shot what may be the most compelling photograph in the entire collection, an old woman looking skyward, with a beatific look on her face, as though she sees the *Gates of Heaven*. In another picture, she is surrounded by several grandchildren sitting on the porch in *Lazy Summer Days*. The rest of our time in Vicksburg was spent shooting mansions, paddleboats, Catfish Row the inside and outside of the Old Courthouse and, finally, a group of World War II veterans at a VFW club.

Along with the compelling photographs that were taken throughout the Mississippi Delta, we were fortunate enough to interview nearly thirty people from all walks of life, different ethnicities, social classes, and backgrounds who were willing to share their knowledge of the past and their hopes for the future. When we interviewed them, our goal, as *always,* was to provide a place for people to speak whose voices might not otherwise be heard. What we wanted to capture was the way ordinary folks talk about their hopes, dreams, and fears—and some of their disappointments. Their stories remind us the Delta isn't stuck in a particular time or place, where bad memories, history, and dark images forever hold residents captive. Instead, it is populated by dynamic people, men and women whose individual stories, when combined, reveal a powerful sense of collective agency—one they use to transform their lives in the face of cultural and economic challenges.

Each voice describes one small part of the Delta's diverse identity, which, when added together, presents as broad a view of the region as we could provide. For both me and Jean-Philippe, whose backgrounds and interests inevitably shape our work, the voices on the recordings, and the images captured on film, allow us to share our vision of the Mississippi Delta, one that we viewed through a wide-angled lens.

Part III, Voices of the Delta, then, is the centerpiece of the book, where people from all walks of life, many from original homelands far away from the area, and from different cultural and ethnic groups, discuss their connection to the Mississippi Delta, the land they all call home. There you will encounter doctors and casino workers, preachers and musicians, teachers, and catfish farmers, and just about everyone in between.

In addition to Jean-Philippe's images—throughout the text and in two powerful photographic essays in parts II and IV—and the informants' powerful stories, we also wanted to include longer interpretative essays that would provide the reader with a guide to important themes of the region's history and culture. Toward this end, actor Morgan Freeman generously allowed himself to be recruited to write a foreword for the book, entitled "My Mississippi Delta Story." Freeman's essay recounts his personal history as a child of the Delta, and he frankly discusses why he is pulled back to his ancestral home, despite its challenges.

In Part I, Delta Memories, Patti Carr Black's wonderful essay, "The Real Delta: Cultural Landmarks," reveals the cultural secrets held captive by the region's fields and swamps, and how that history of pain and misery was transformed into an art form unique to the Delta—the blues. Christine Wilson's essay, "Highway 61: Lifeline of the Delta," explores that art form in depth, from one end of the Delta to the other.

Part V, A Delta Dream, is a complement to the introductory essays. It begins with Nikki Giovanni's stirring, gritty tribute poem "Boiled Blues (for the

Mississippi Delta)," which Giovanni kindly composed for this volume. Writer Robin Rushing's "Growing Up in Indianola" provides the valuable point of view of a young white girl who was forced to confront racial issues when she sees Civil Rights marchers in her own town, on her own street and, finally, in her own yard. Later, she is forced to confront her own feelings, when her school, her local restaurant, and her theater are integrated. Most importantly, she tells the reader how all these events made her face her feelings about Dora, her family's African American housekeeper and Robin's surrogate mother.

Mississippi state senator and Civil Rights giant David Jordan contributes "It's Hard to Beat a Made-Up Mind." This magnificent autobiographical piece documents his own personal struggle to achieve equality for both himself and his younger fellow citizens in Greenwood. His choice of weapons for this life-long battle were the U.S. Federal Courts and the local ballot box. Jordan's piece, while filled with hope, is a reminder of victories won and struggles that still lay ahead.

What then of the last, most important thing we were looking for—the heart of the Delta—the one thing that turns our slow moving caterpillar into a beautiful butterfly? I think I found the Delta's heart in a story told by a white middle aged man one evening as he stared into the bayou and reminisced about a Martin Luther King visit to the Delta:

> He could speak like no one I'd ever heard before. There was something in his voice that's hard to describe. When he came to speak in Clarksdale, me and two of my buddies got in an old pickup truck and armed ourselves with slingshots and marbles. We were going to get on the street next to where he was speaking, shoot the marbles over the roof, and disrupt the crowd. But when we were safely hidden, in the alley on the next street, he was already speaking, and we could hear his voice over the PA system; it was different from anything I had ever heard before. As we sat there on that bench, he spoke, and we listened, and he spoke some more, and we listened some more, and when he finished speaking, we laid down our slingshots and our marbles on the bench, and we got up, crawled into the truck, and went home.

When I asked him how he felt about what had happened, he paused a long time, then said, "I don't know how I felt, but I know we didn't shoot any marbles."

As far as I was concerned, after four decades of traveling into the Delta, what I had been looking for had literally fallen into my lap—living proof that the past could be remembered and the future could be embraced without fear or violence. I honestly believe that our book captures the living, beating heart of the Mississippi Delta, whose thump, thump, thumping sound shows a people determined, when given the chance, to do the right thing, and to tell their own stories, in their own words, defining themselves, not allowing themselves to be defined by others. *Highway 61: Heart of the Delta* documents their struggle. We applaud all their efforts, and salute each of their successes!

Randall Norris

*"The Mississippi Delta stretches from the lobby of the
Peabody Hotel, to Catfish Row in Vicksburg."*

Courtesy of David L. Cohn

**Doorman
The Peabody Hotel
Memphis**

**Catfish Row
Vicksburg**

Part One

DELTA MEMORIES

Delta Highway
Highway 61 South

The Real Delta: Cultural Landmarks

Patti Carr Black

In geographical terms the Mississippi River Delta includes 308 counties in Illinois, Kentucky, Missouri, Tennessee, Arkansas, Louisiana, and Mississippi. But in legendary terms, the Mississippi Delta indisputably means the small crescent of land in northwest Mississippi known as the Yazoo-Mississippi Delta—usually simply called the Delta—which David Cohn described as beginning "in the lobby of the Peabody Hotel in Memphis and ending on Catfish Row in Vicksburg."

Within its eleven counties and five partial counties, a distinct culture has formed. Four million acres of rich alluvial land in the interior of the Delta, at one time impenetrable, were made available through building levees, draining the swamps, cutting the forests, and laying railroads.

The cotton kingdom moved upriver from the Natchez area to the new rich land, where cotton became an obsession and a way of life. It created a great deal of wealth for Delta landowners and merchants and hard times for African Americans who also moved upriver to provide the major labor in the cotton fields. After slavery, their labor was kept cheap through the sharecropping system, in effect a new kind of slavery, which victimized the poor—black and white alike.

Despite this backdrop, or perhaps because of it, this Delta is the land where the blues—the seminal music of the twentieth century—was born. This music is the precursor of jazz, rhythm and blues, and rock. From the Delta's flatland towns have come prize-winning playwrights and novelists, like Tennessee Williams and Eudora Welty. But round and through its well-ordered cotton fields, lavish wilderness still reigns. Its people, more ethnically varied than most other parts of the state, have endured each other's animosity and moved along with each other's generosity. Major immigrant groups, many descended from people brought in to meet labor needs, include Chinese, Italian, Lebanese, Jewish, Greek, Mexican and, representing more than half the population, those who trace their heritage to Africa.

Today the Delta is still a land of extreme poverty and wealth: a land that struggles with high unemployment, low incomes, and underfunded public schools. It is a land that is still mostly agricultural, where rice, soybeans, corn, and catfish vie with cotton as the most valuable crop, and the labor force has mainly been supplanted, if not virtually replaced, by farm mechanization. It is a land still crippled by vestiges of segregation but brought together by the hope of cultural tourism, which is focusing on Delta blues and its practitioners.

Highway 61 flows through the Delta almost like a mobius strip curving from the past as it merges into the future and leads the present back to the past. It is a historic route for African Americans. It was an escape from Jim Crow laws to the freedom in the North. It was the path to better economic opportunities in the 1920s and 1940s, leading to jobs in Detroit, Chicago, St. Louis, and other cities "up north." Highway 61 was called the "chitlin' circuit" by bluesmen of the 1920s and 1930s, playing in juke joints up and down the strip. And it was the route for Delta bluesmen who migrated to Chicago and created urban blues with its distinctive electric guitar—among the creators of this music were the Delta's own Muddy Waters from Rolling Fork, Willie Dixon from Vicksburg, B. B. King from Indianola, Sonny Boy Williamson II from Glendora, and Howlin' Wolf, who had worked at the Dockery Plantation.

During its two-hundred-mile leg through the Delta, Highway 61 passes most of the Delta's illustrious sites. Major cultural attractions flash by: storied juke joints and blues clubs, roadside art, homes of famous writers, sites of blues festivals, cafes with old-time southern cooking, and an increasing number of museums dedicated to the blues, and natural areas that preserve wilderness past.

Leaving the lobby of the Peabody Hotel in Memphis and heading south, a single side trip can attest to the impact that Delta blues has had on the world of music: visit Graceland, Elvis Presley's home in south Memphis. Presley's producer, Sam Phillips, was first attracted to Presley because "he sings Negro rhythms with a white voice." Elvis Presley recorded songs by Delta bluesmen Arthur "Big Boy" Crudup, Rufus Thomas, Little Junior Parker, and others, and he focused national attention on the blues. Later, rock musicians sought the same source. The Rolling Stones, Eric Clapton, John Lennon, and Bob Dylan have all acknowledged the influence of Delta bluesmen on their music.

Heading south from Memphis into the Delta, the first site is atypical, almost surrealistic: Casino Row in Tunica. Some dozen casinos seem to rise like a phantasmagoria up from the cotton fields. Required by law to be on water, the casinos skate the letter of the law with small unseen ponds at their base. (Farther down the river, casinos in Vicksburg and Natchez are literally floating on the Mississippi River.) The Horseshoe Casino in Tunica, cashing in on local color, features The Blues and Legends Hall of Fame Museum, with artifacts and exhibits on Mississippi blues greats Muddy Waters and John Lee Hooker, along with Muddy Waters's pupil, Eric Clapton. On Highway 61 at Tunica, the first taste of down-home cooking is available at such eateries as the Blue and White Café, The Hollywood Café, and Mama's Best (which features turnip greens, chitterlings, hog maws, and cornbread).

From Tunica south, the variety of cultural riches becomes apparent. At the little town of Rich, the old studio of Thomas Harris still stands. Novelist Harris is

best known for *The Silence of the Lambs,* but his work includes *Black Sunday, Red Dragon,* and *Hannibal*—all made into major movies. Harris grew up in Rich and returned there to write. A short side trip from Rich, two miles on Highway 49 West to Moon Lake, yields another literary site. Uncle Henry's Place and Inn on the lake was once known as the Moon Lake Casino, a notorious gambling and dance hall during Prohibition, immortalized in fiction by Eudora Welty and in drama by Tennessee Williams.

Beyond Moon Lake is the first opportunity to see the Mississippi River, which forms the western boundary of the Delta. Three bridges in the Delta cross the river: at Vicksburg, Greenville, and here where the bridge crosses to Helena, Arkansas. The Mississippi River—celebrated in folklore, fiction, films, and Broadway musicals—is now busy with tugboats, barges, and flat-bottom boats that carry coal, forest products, petroleum, sand, gravel, iron ore, grains, and manufactured products. Tourism has brought back a passenger steamboat or two, with their calliopes playing "Are You from Dixie?"

The Mississippi River is also one of the most diverse fisheries in the world. With over 183 species of fish, it has commercial and sport fishing galore. Its numerous tributaries snake through the Delta, and the woods of the bottomland

and provide the means for the Delta's favorite pastimes: fishing, hunting, camping, picnicking, and hiking. The abundance of wetlands adjacent to the river make the Delta the central core of the Mississippi Flyway, a migratory course that teal and mallard ducks (among other birds) travel between South and North America. Hunting clubs abound in the Delta, from those that require expensive memberships to lean-to camps for seasonal activity: hunting deer, wild turkeys, quail, rabbits, squirrels, and ducks. Back on Highway 61, the road continues south to Clarksdale, the epicenter of the blues boom in the Delta.

Housed in the old Clarksdale railroad depot is the Delta Blues Museum, which exhibits Muddy Waters's cabin from the old Stovall Plantation. One of the nation's first blues stations, WROX Radio, is still on the air. Juke joints are freewheeling and soul food can be found at many cafés. Street names include Blues Alley and John Lee Hooker Lane. Issaquena and Sunflower Avenues are rife with blues sites and historical markers, including one for W. C. Handy, who came to Clarksdale for two years to teach members of the Negro Knights of Pythias Band. The Empress of the Blues, Bessie Smith, who was in a car accident on Highway 61, died in Clarksdale's black hospital. The structure still exists as the Riverside Hotel. Morgan Freeman, award-winning actor and native Mississippian, and his partners Bill Luckett and Howard Stovall, have rejuvenated the Clarksdale scene with the opening of Ground Zero Blues Club, and Madidi, a gourmet restaurant.

No one can doubt that blues represent a potent type of literature, and every October Clarksdale celebrates its other literary claims. The Tennessee Williams Festival presents plays performed on the front porches of historic homes. Williams lived here and later visited the home of his grandfather, Walter Dakin, an Episcopal minister. The rectory still stands, and locals can point to other structures and families that influenced Williams's great works of the American theatre. (For example, his next-door neighbor kept a collection of glass animals in her window.) The Tennessee Williams Park features the angel from *Summer and Smoke*.

Clarksdale is also the birthplace of Lerone Bennett, son of a chauffeur and cook, who became a noted author and long-time editor of *Ebony* magazine. He was also a clarinet and sax player. Two other staples of southern food are

Duck Season
Ryan Rawlings
Tutwiler

available in Clarksdale at Abe's Bar-B-Q on Highway 61 and Hicks Superette on Fifth Street where Bill Clinton and Jesse Jackson sampled the hot tamales, an import that came when Mexican workers were brought in to chop and pick cotton in the 1930s.

Continuing south through the cotton fields, Highway 61 sweeps by Mound Bayou, one of the oldest African American towns in the United States. The City Hall has a carved bas relief featuring Malcolm X, Martin Luther King Jr., and Fannie Lou Hamer, a field hand and courageous worker for civil rights, whose famous statement before Congress is often quoted: "I am sick and tired of being sick and tired."

The visual arts are abundant in the Delta in a variety of media. Along Highway 61, Peter's Pottery in Mound Bayou, operated by Peter Woods and his brothers, is one of the first sites of visual arts activity. Five miles down the road in Marigold is the famous McCarty Pottery and Gardens. Five miles farther, Cleveland has the liveliest sculptor in the state, Floyd Shaman, whose outsized work is satiric in tone and created with consummate workmanship, while Delta State University has a coterie of well-known plein air artists—a group dedicated to painting in the open air—at work.

A marker on the grounds of the Bolivar County Courthouse notes that W. C. Handy often played for the Bogue Phalia Outing Club of Cleveland and first played the blues for whites at a dance here. The courthouse also holds Charley Patton's applications for four marriage licenses (out of a total of eight). Cleveland's annual events are the Crosstie Arts Festival and October Fest; the latter features a barbecue cook-off.

Abe's Bar-B-Q
Clarksdale

Straight down to Leland on Highway 61, the cultural tone expands. Here is The Birthplace of the Frog, a museum honoring Leland native Jim Henson, creator of the muppets. Blues, nonetheless, permeates the town where James "Son Ford" Thomas, Little Milton, Willie Foster, Boogaloo Ames, Jimmy Reed, Eddie Cusic, and others are honored with a mural on Fourth Street. Leland also has the state's only monument to football, one of the Delta's leading distractions. An elegant 1936 sculpture of a football player at the Leland High School stadium is by artist Joseph Barras.

An obligatory side trip off Highway 61 is the ten miles from Leland to Greenville. For decades, Greenville was the cultural core of the Delta, once boasting the true fact that it had more writers per square foot than any city its size. Contemporary writers Shelby Foote, Walker Percy, Ellen Douglas, Hodding Carter Jr., Hodding Carter III, and Beverly Lowry all called it home. Today, Greenville has riverboat casinos on the waterfront and blues clubs along Nelson and Walnut streets. The blues "Walk of Fame" is on Walnut Street. The most famous eatery in the state is Doe's Eat Place on Nelson Street, which was once a juke joint and café, and now is a still grungy restaurant crowded with fans of

**Lawnmower Army
Vicksburg National
Military Park**

**Then and Now
Park Ranger
Vicksburg National
Military Park**

its enormous beef steaks and hot tamales. A short detour some four miles east of Cleveland is Dockery Farms, the famous home base of blues musicians in the 1920s and 1930s, the plantation where the blues may have first been played. Charley Patton grew up there and attracted other blues players to the area, notably Robert Johnson and Howlin' Wolf. The Peavine Railroad, a local branch line, was here and inspired Patton's "Peavine Blues."

Greenville hosts the annual Mississippi Delta Blues and Heritage Festival, the Little Wynn Blues Festival, and the Delta Wildlife Expo. The Leroy Percy State Park, Mississippi's oldest and largest, is just outside Greenville on Highway 12, and Winterville Mounds, a significant pre-Columbian site, is nearby on Highway 1 North. The Delta was a pristine home for the Native Americans of Mississippi, both those who have lived here since 4000 BC, and the most recent arrivals. For several hundred years the Choctaw and Chickasaw tribes hunted wild game here and made long trips on foot to gather materials to make their baskets.

The last leg of Highway 61 through the Delta goes from Leland to Vicksburg passing by a series of towns with exotic-sounding names: Arcola, Hollandale, Panther Burn, Nitta Yuma, Anguilla, Rolling Fork, Cary, and Onward.

At Onward, a historic marker reminds the traveler of the Delta's dense wilderness that was drained and cleared to make way for the flat fields where cotton and soybeans once flourished, and ponds where catfish now grow. The marker tells the story of Theodore Roosevelt, who visited the area on a hunting trip. Guided by a famous local African American hunter, Holt Collier, Roosevelt declined to shoot a bear that had been cornered for him and thereby set off the creation of the manufactured "Teddy Bear," still an icon of America's childhood. Just east of Onward is the massive Delta National Forest, which stretches almost to Yazoo City. A National Natural Landmark, it contains rare remnants of the virgin bottomland hardwood forests where bears, wolves, and panthers once roamed.

Vicksburg marks the base of the fabled Delta. As you approach the city, Margaret's Grocery stretches a hundred feet or more along Highway 61, the work of Rev. H. D. Dennis, who had the grocery and the red, white, and blue masonry towers built as a gift to his wife. Vicksburg is preeminently a Civil War site. To be sure, other Delta towns commemorate the Confederate dead—there are courthouse monuments in Cleveland, Greenwood, Sumner, Vicksburg, Yazoo City, and Greenville—but the Vicksburg National Military Park draws tens of thousands yearly to its somber grounds. The Union army lay siege to Vicksburg for forty-eight days in 1863 for control of the Mississippi River. Fierce battles led to many casualties before the Union captured the city, and in 1899 the park was established to commemorate the lives of fallen soldiers from both the Confederate and Union armies.

There are 1,200 monuments and memorials on those 1,323 acres, making it the largest collection of outdoor sculpture in the nation. The Jacqueline House African American Museum, also in Vicksburg, houses artifacts, photographs, and audio/visual collections. The Old Court House, built in 1858 with skilled slave labor working from plans drawn up by an African American, is now a Museum of Civil War and Warren County history. The building, an archetype of antebellum architecture, was the Warren County courthouse until 1940 and served as a hospital during the Civil War siege of Vicksburg.

Vicksburg also has its musical claims. It is the birthplace of sweet-voiced bluesman Skip James, who played all over the Delta and was rediscovered in the 1960s revival of interest in blues. It is also the hometown of Willie Dixon, one of the most prolific songwriters during the rise of urban blues. He wrote over two hundred hits for Mississippi's Chicago performers, including Muddy Waters, Howlin' Wolf, Little Walter, Otis Rush, and Bo Diddley. He wrote rock songs for Elvis Presley, Chuck Berry, Van Morrison, Eric Clapton, and the Allman Brothers Band.

The Delta is culturally rich beyond the towns along Highway 61. Other nationally known writers from the Delta include Ellen Gilchrist of Issaquena County; Willie Morris of Yazoo City; Clifton Taulbert, Glen Allen, Lewis Nordan, all from Itta Bena; Endesha Ida Mae Holland and Donna Tart of Greenwood. Greenwood also has the Cottonlandia Museum, Florewood River Plantation State Park, the Cotton Capital Blues Festival, and the annual Delta Band Festival, featuring over a hundred marching bands; Indianola is the hometown of B. B. King, who gives a homecoming concert there every year; Yazoo City has the Oakes African American Cultural Center; Belzoni is the home of the Catfish Museum and Mama's Dream World, a museum which features Ethel Wright Mohamed's stitchery: pictures of her memories of the Mississippi Delta. Finally, there is Parch-

The Greatest
Generation
WW II Veterans of
Foreign Wars

man Farm, site of the famous and infamous state penitentiary, a catalyst for blues lyrics, like those of Bukka White:

> Oh, listen you men, I don't mean no harm (2X)
> If you wanna do good, you better stay off old Parchman Farm.
> We go to work in the mornin' just at dawn of day (2X)
> Just at the setting of the sun, that's when work is done.
> I'm down on Parchman Farm, but I sho' wanna go back home
> And I hope someday I will overcome good,
> you better stay off old Parchman Farm.
> We got to work in the mornin' just at dawn of day (2X)
> Just at the setting of the sun, that's when work is done.
> I'm down on Parchman Farm, but I sho' wanna go back home
> And I hope someday I will overcome.

William Faulkner may be right. This land has shaped the people, the traditions, the culture and the character of the Delta. Faulkner described the Delta in *Go Down, Moses:* "In the beginning, it was virgin—to the west, along the Big Black River, the alluvial swamps threaded by black, almost motionless bayous and impenetrable with cane and buck vine and cypress and ash and oak and gum. . . . This land, this South . . . with woods for game and streams for fish and deep rich soil for seed and lush springs to sprout it and long summers to mature it and serene falls to harvest it and short mild winters for men and animals. That's the trouble with this country. Everything, weather, all, hangs on too long. Like our rivers, our land: is opaque, slow, violent, shaping and creating the life of man in its implacable and brooding image."

The Crossroads

Clarksdale

Highway 61: Lifeline of the Delta

Christine Wilson

If you grew up in western Mississippi, you might take Highway 61 for granted. It's the road you took to parties in any number of nearby Delta towns; the road to Memphis to shop; or the scenic drive south to the so-called Key to the Confederacy, Vicksburg, through River Country to Washington, first capital of the Mississippi Territory, and on to Natchez, the oldest settlement on the Mississippi River.

Some people don't take it for granted. Visitors to Highway 61 revel in its atmosphere, and they bathe in the humid air, soaking up the feeling to remember it; they lovingly take in the lay of the land, the particular and changing light along the road as it meanders from the bright northern Delta to the deep shade of southern Mississippi's out-of-control vegetation. A road is a thing of hope, and this road is a particular gift—a road unlike any they have traveled.

Blues fans are especially in awe of it, and why not? Along this road, or near it, was produced the most compelling blues music in America—blues, the foundation of American music. How did this great art form come to be created in a place like this, in this part of the world? There is no one answer to that old question, but here are some of the reasons.

First, blacks and whites lived and worked in close proximity in a poor state—and even before it was a state—where music was the central leisure activity for both. It created a rich mix of instruments, traditions, personalities, rhythms. Blacks lived around large plantations across the Delta, which together served as a network for musicians who traveled among them, sharing and borrowing music, until different styles of the blues appeared around the state. Blues music could be played on a harmonica (harp) or a cheap guitar, and the chord progression, at its root, was fairly simple and easy to pick up. You didn't have to read music. The style was improvisatory; you didn't have to play it any certain way.

Another part is that there was a stimulating, often frightening, environment in Mississippi, especially on its western front, near Highway 61, where there were floods, tornadoes, storms, intense heat, and drought, bringing destruction, death, change, and renewal—and there is a vital connection between environment and imagination. The environment also offered an abundantly green, fertile, and wild landscape, dotted with burial mounds built by an earlier people and full of names evocative of the heritage of the Old South and its larger-than-life heroes, setting the stage for more of the same and creating a climate in

A Cup of Soup
Rosewood

which an ordinary working man like John Henry or a blues singer like Robert Johnson could become a folk hero for all time.

Near Highway 61 was also the Mississippi River, a beacon on the landscape. Even for those who had never laid eyes on it, it was a large symbol of hope, an escape to something better, a tangible and vast open highway that they knew was there. The mixing that created the blues began when slaves introduced their African ways to a land they were unwillingly brought to—a central part of their African heritage was music. Blacks did, over the centuries, adopt genres of the Western musical tradition they heard around them: country dance tunes, folk songs, narrative ballads, and hymns. But the strong rhythms and emotions of African music were ingrained, part of their way of dealing with the world. Denied the use of drums by their owners, slaves would develop substitutes: rhythmic wailing and clapping in spirituals and gospel, the strumming and beating of a cheap western guitar.

They adapted the Western scale, bending its notes to produce a music that was exceptionally expressive, intimate, and intense—music unlike anything Anglo-Americans had ever heard. Since those days when the blues was born in the Delta or some place like it, blues has become part of the American (and world) psyche. That mix of major and minor keys and inflections resonated, touched a deep chord. It seemed to express the human condition. The blues expressed a kind of truth.

From musical gatherings on plantations near Highway 61, like Dockery Farms, came rhythms, lyrics, bass patterns, and guitar riffs that spread throughout the world, influencing many styles, from pop to jazz to country, classical,

**Harpman
Frank "Jelly Roll" Frost
Lula**

and rock. What is an appropriate word to describe the number of important blues musicians that were born along this route, or nearby? Unbelievable, statistically impossible, maybe even miraculous. But to make the point, here is a brief (and incomplete) list of outstanding musicians—listed in alphabetical order—that were born in towns on or near this road.

Guitarist *Johnnie Billington,* born in Crowder, settled in Clarksdale, where he teaches young people about the blues; *Charlie Booker* also hails from Sunflower County. The great *Big Bill Broonzy,* born in Scott, went to Chicago and became one of the most popular performers in the country. Bluesman *Robert Brown* was born in the little town of Itta Bena, Choctaw words meaning "home in the woods." *Willie Brown* is also from the Clarksdale brood. Harp player *Little George Buford* was born in Hernando. Crooner *Jerry Butler* ("For Your Precious Love" and others) was born in Sunflower (near Indianola) and made his name in Chicago.

Little Milton Campbell, born near Inverness, moved from Sun to Stax to Malaco labels. Chicago jazz and blues favorite *Jeanne Carroll* was born in Hernando. Pioneer *Sam Chatmon* of the Mississippi Sheiks is from Bolton but lived and played in Hollandale. Indianola claims *Louis "Bo" Collins* of later Detroit fame. Clarksdale produced the iconic *Sam Cooke,* who set standards that are yet to be surpassed. Tunica gave us *James Cotton,* master harpist, and Greenville produced pop/soul/blues artist *Tyrone Davis. James "Peck" Curtis,* a King Biscuit regular, is from Benoit, and blues/jazz great *Olu Dara* was brought to us by the city of Natchez.

Robert Diggs of Friars Point played with the Sheiks in Hollandale. Often called the Granddaddy of the blues, *Willie Dixon* grew up in Vicksburg, while *David "Honeyboy" Edwards,* another Chicago great, came out of Shaw.

C. L. Franklin, father of Aretha and an influence on countless blues/gospel musicians, was born in Indianola and lived and preached in Clarksdale. Delta blues player *Willie Foster* of Greenville is buried in Indianola, the town harp player *William "Jazz" Gillum* hailed from, and *Boyd Gilmore* came out of Drew, as did Chicago musician *Homer Harris. Milt "The Judge" Hinton* of Vicksburg played jazz bass—rooted in blues—the world over. Blues giant *John Lee Hooker* was another of the Clarksdale issue, and *Big Walter Horton* was born just up the road at Horn Lake. Leland, a little south, produced R&B star *Thelma Houston.*

Luther "Guitar" Johnson came out of Itta Bena and the seminal figure *Eddie "Guitar Slim" Jones* is from Greenwood. The venerable *Mississippi John Hurt* was born in Teoc but sang about his adopted hometown of Avalon, near Greenwood. *Hank Jones* is another jazz great from Vicksburg, and blues master *Albert King* was born and bred in Indianola, as was the other famous *King, B. B.,* now called the King of the Blues.

Clayton Love of Clarksdale and *Willie Love* of Duncan contributed greatly to Mississippi blues, as did *Albert "Sunnyland Slim" Luandrew* of Vance and *James McCoy* of Drew. Blues great *Fred McDowell* was a product of Como, and *Hayes B. McMullen* was from up the road in Tutwiler.

Keepin' the Blues Alive
Bill "Howl-N-Madd" Perry
Ground Zero Blues Club
Clarksdale

Jazz/blues great *Mulgrew Miller* was born in Greenwood. Blues giant *McKinley "Muddy Waters" Morganfield* was born in Rolling Fork and spent time in Clarksdale before moving north. And yet another blues giant—*Aleck "Rice" Miller, a.k.a., "Sonny Boy Williamson II"*—was brought to us by the town of Glendora. Guitarist *Johnnie B. Moore* and R&B great *Junior Parker* were two more from Clarksdale. Greenville gave us *Jimmy Phillips* and *Eugene Powell*, and Leland gave us the R&B superstar *Jimmy Reed*.

Fenton Robinson came out of Minter City, and *Jimmy Rogers*, guitarist for *Muddy Waters*, was from Ruleville. *Oliver Sain* came up in Dundee, *Brother John Sellers* was from Clarksdale, *and Henry "Son" Sims*, of Clarksdale, fiddled with *Charley Patton*. Lots of Smiths started playing the blues along Highway 61: *Albert Smith* of Bolivar County, *Leo Smith* of Leland, *Moses Smith* of Jefferson County, and *Willie Mae Ford Smith* of Rolling Fork. *Houston Stackhouse* was from Wesson. The world-famous *Staples Singers* (led by *Roebuck "Pop" Staples*) were a product of Drew, Mississippi; *Napoleon Strickland* came from Como. *Theodore R. "Hound Dog" Taylor* was a Natchez native, and *"Doc" Terry* grew up in Sunflower County.

James "Son" Thomas of Leland became a revered bluesman and folk artist. Rocker *Ike Turner* was from Clarksdale. *John "Big Moose" Walker* was born

Christine Wilson

in Washington County, and *Peewee Whittaker* in Natchez. *Nelson "Dirty Red" Wilborn* came up in Tallahatchie County, and *Big Joe Williams* was a product of Crawford.

Joseph "Jo Jo" Williams was born in Coahoma, and *Mary Wilson* (of the Supremes) in Greenville. *Johnny Young,* Chicago blues mandolin player, grew up in Vicksburg, and he once remarked: "I grew up in Vicksburg, so I heard all them guys. Even Charley Patton." Finally, jazz great *Lester Young*, dubbed Prez, grew up way down at the southern end of Highway 61, in Woodville.

Other great blues artists, like *Charley Patton, Robert Johnson,* and *Tommy Johnson,* were born a little farther away, but they lost no time in making their way up Highway 61 to gigs on the plantation network, play parties, and juke joints.

Highway 61 was many things to the African Americans living in the Delta during the last century. It was the road that many took to escape Mississippi and the conditions of life here. It served others as a lifeline, connecting them to family, to jobs, to the music that sustained them. Musicians traveled this road to find other kindred souls and to find audiences to nurture them and their music. Some saw the highway—and its crossroads—as a life-changing place, as a metaphor for the place where the artist must go, alone, to test his or her commitment to the art. Highway 61 looms large over Mississippi symbolically, meaning many things to many people, but most of all it carries the idea of hope—and of possibilities yet undreamed.

Horseshoe Casino Tunica

Part Two

PEOPLE, PLACES, THINGS:
A PHOTO ESSAY

Night Train • Mikoma Crossing

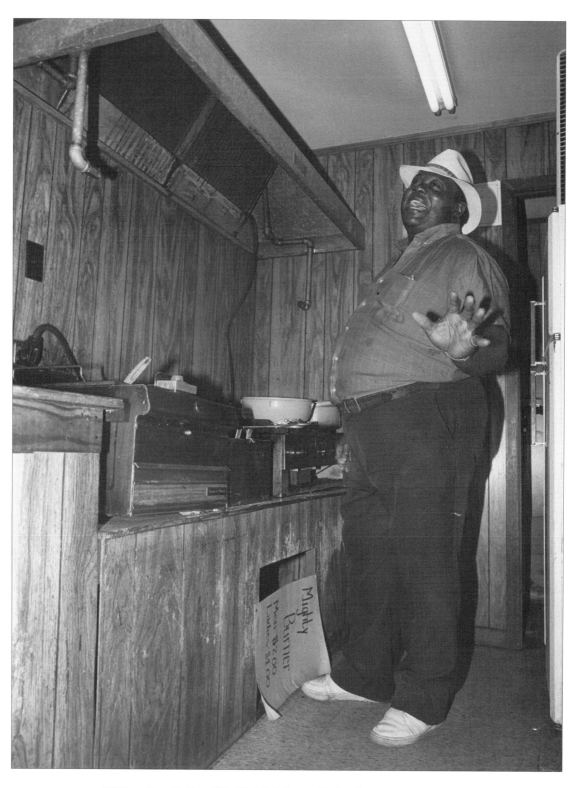

All You Can Eat! • "Catfish" John • Delta Avenue Blues Club

Homage • Aleck "Sonny Boy Williamson II" Miller • Wrightman Cemetery • Tutwiler

Sleeping Sentinels • Honey Hill Plantation • Highway 61

Hobo's Cadillac • Cleveland

Vicksburg National Military Cemetery

Waiting to Load • Greenwood

Carpenter's Hammer • Amos Harper • Clarksdale

Mr. And Mrs. Jang • Chinese Grocery Store Owners • Shaw

Next! • Sandy D'Angelo • Greenville

Elders • Antioch AME Church • Sumner

Gates of Heaven • Woman at the Back Gate • Vicksburg National Cemetery

Part Three

VOICES OF THE DELTA

*"I thank you Lord that my layin' down bed was not my coolin' off board,
and that the walls of my room were not the walls of my tomb."*

Sunday Morning Gospel Hour • WROX 1450 AM • Clarksdale

Steve Stewart

Former Editor • Clarksdale Press Register • Clarksdale

A good community newspaper must be both the community's biggest booster while at the same time being its most objective critic. The notion that a newspaper should only be a cheerleader and ignore the community's problems is wrong. I think good community newspapers, like ours, are quick to praise those efforts and those people who are worthy of praise, but the paper is also not afraid to confront those issues and problems that hold the community back. I have observed cases over the years where the newspaper in a community was a real driving force, where it was instrumental in a community succeeding. That does not mean being a cheerleader and a mouthpiece for the chamber of commerce, even though we are actively involved with, and fully support, the efforts of our local chamber of commerce. Its members are our advertisers, and sometimes we have to praise and criticize them, even within the pages of a single issue. We do, however, try to be responsible in our criticism, which allows us to be a crucial ingredient in a successful town. I've done the tour of the Delta, from the southern tip at Yazoo City to Clarksdale on the northern end, and I can honestly say that the Delta has truly become my home.

The Delta is a fascinating place culturally. Its people are some of the most interesting people I have ever encountered. It's as culturally diverse a region as I think you'll find anywhere; on the borders of a single county, you will find some of our nation's most impoverished people living within a mile of some of the nation's wealthiest planters. For me, that just makes for a very, very interesting cultural mix. At the same time, however, I do think that kind of diversity is often conducive to conflict. I don't mean conflict at a personal level but at an institutional one. There's always been, more or less, a naturally adversarial relationship between the press and governmental leaders. That's certainly the case in Washington, D.C., and it's no different in Clarksdale, Mississippi, here in the Mississippi Delta. I go to church with and sit in the pew behind some of the politicians I occasionally criticize. In Washington, and even bigger cities like New York and Chicago, newspapers tend to be a little more insulated from the institutions and people they cover. In Clarksdale, that situation has been particularly difficult, since the younger political leaders have taken over from the older ones.

Clarksdale, more so than the other Delta towns I have lived in and observed closely as a journalist, has had, for the most part over the years, responsible leadership. Our elected officials here have a pretty good history of cooperating

"Some of the old stalwarts, like Aaron Henry, have passed on. He was very soft spoken, and he always sought responsible, peaceful solutions to problems."

with one another, especially along racial lines. Some of the old stalwarts, particularly in the black community, like Aaron Henry, have passed on.

Dr. Henry was one of the great civil rights leaders in Mississippi. He was a pharmacist, a long-time state legislator, and a successful businessman. Dr. Henry was unwavering in his fight for equal opportunity and civil rights, and he never compromised his principals. He was very soft spoken, and he always sought responsible, peaceful solutions to problems. He didn't scream and shout and pound podiums. But he was very effective, because people respected him in both the black and white communities. Unfortunately, that has all changed. Even though each new generation here has become more enlightened about race and class, an interesting phenomenon, especially in the black community, has occurred.

The newest generation of black political leadership, in my view, tends to operate with a little sharper edge than the preceding generation. I think, however, that rather than being issue-oriented as it was in the past, it has become personality driven, and subsequently the whole process, particularly Clarksdale's city government, is filled with acrimony and conflict. Politically, we have a four ward system, with a mayor elected citywide. The mayor's vote is only one of five, so it could be called a weak mayoral system. The mayor is African American, as are two of the commissioners, so we currently have a three to two African American split on the council. In some situations, when the paper has addressed problems that needed a solution, the paper and the council's majority have been at odds, and that has caused some politicians not to like us.

That's all right, however, because the citizenry is very supportive of the newspaper, and of our obligation to report and comment on the good and the bad. And there's so much good! We don't have to bend over backwards to find the good, positive stories. I'm in the Delta because I like it. I like its people and its institutions. I happen to find some of the problems fascinating and interesting from a journalist's perspective. What journalist would want to live in a place where there are no problems or conflict and nothing interesting to analyze? For instance, one of the major problems we have in Clarksdale is how to improve the local school system.

I think schools are a major factor in the overall decline of the population, particularly the middle class, both black and white. A quick glance at the demographics shows that we haven't just been affected by black flight, but we have been affected by white flight as well, and a lot of that flight has been because of the schools. The school system is, of course, very sensitive to criticism because we have some extremely hard-working administrators and teachers, including my wife, in our educational community. Unfortunately, however, they are fighting an uphill battle because we demand too much from the school system. The fact of the matter is that if you look at all of the standards by which schools are judged, including standardized test scores, our public schools in the Delta are not doing well. And that is a turn off to middle-class families who cannot afford private school tuition.

They are not going to stay in an area with substandard public education, not when they can move fifty miles away and be in a very successful, high performing public school district. Upgrading the quality of the public schools will be a huge factor in improving the demographics for the entire community. We can upgrade the system by turning parental apathy into parental involvement, where parents attend PTA meetings, help their kids with their homework, and bake a cake or pie for the annual bake sale; in short, becoming actively involved in their children's lives. This will help create a sense of community.

One day I discovered that in the newspaper business we often use the word "community" very loosely. We use it simply to define a group of people living within a geographic boundary, but I believe the true meaning of community is when people of like mind and like heart come together and cooperate on matters that benefit everyone. There's an Episcopal priest in Greenville, Mississippi, Liz Jones, who is very involved with the Mastery Foundation, an international nonprofit group that has a history of building a sense of community. When we contacted the Mastery Foundation, we discovered that they had worked extensively in northern Ireland, Israel, and the Middle East. I said, "My goodness, the Delta should be a cake walk compared to Northern Ireland." Reverend Jones believes, as I do, that the same kind of work was desperately needed in the Delta. We decided that for too long in the Delta the elected and political leadership has set the tone for interaction between people in the community, and that tone has not always been positive. So we decided to set the tone ourselves. Last year, in August, we sponsored the first of what we hope to be an annual Clarksdale Community Empowerment Conference.

The conference brought together a group of fifty people of great racial, professional, and economic diversity. They gathered at Carnegie Public Library in Clarksdale for two days, where they literally locked the doors and began to talk. They didn't really tackle any specific problems or address individual agendas; it was all about creating a dialogue that had not previously existed. We were wildly successful because the benefits occurred in real time. The benefit was in the dialogue. We didn't get consumed with the ultimate outcome. We simply discussed everyone's hopes and fears and put them on a wall and started discussing them one at a time.

We did not encourage participation from elected and political leaders, because there was a concern that the political element might see it as an opportunity to divide and conquer, and we also didn't want members of our own group spending their time and energy throwing rocks and blaming political leaders for our problems. We were concerned that their presence could be harmful to our purpose. We didn't tell them they couldn't participate—we just didn't encourage them to come. What we intended to prove was that there was an active, cooperative citizenry that could make progress and succeed, in spite of the communities' elected and political leadership, rather than because of that leadership.

Since then, we've held a potluck supper in a church fellowship hall, and we've gotten together for a luncheon, but the object is to keep the dialogue going, so we can bring our group back together and look at where we are going with this movement. I really believe it to be a movement. I'm certainly not comparing it to the great civil rights movement of the 1960s, but rather it's a local movement designed to benefit our town and our community. When we feel like we're strong enough, that we've found our purpose, and that we're secure in where we want to go, that's when we'll bring our elected and political leaders to the table. We're trying to do that right now. On Tuesday, we are going to have a luncheon with them, and try to expand the circle. I'm very proud that the Emerick family newspaper chain where I've spent my career, as well as the Clarksdale Press Register, are helping people overcome their chronic inability to cross and break down the Delta's historical barriers regarding race, class, and culture that have separated us for far too long.

Bennie Brown

Community Leader • Jonestown

My father worked hard! He was a sharecropper, a mechanic, a barber, a cobbler, and he even made moonshine. There were fourteen of us, and he did whatever he had to do to keep food on the table. When I finished eighth grade we moved to Jonestown, and Daddy opened a grocery store and a service station. My brothers and I sacked groceries, washed cars, and changed oil. Daddy was the first black constable, and the older boys were on the volunteer fire department. It was rough, but at the time, it didn't seem rough. I actually felt rich; there was always an abundance of food, an abundance of love, and money wasn't a problem, because we all worked. Daddy was a Republican, and he believed in everyone working hard and carrying their fair share of the load. I certainly carried mine; back then it was legal to let black children out of school at noon to work in the fields. My earliest memories are of chopping cotton, but we did other work as well.

Sometimes we'd pick up pecans. We usually got paid ten cents a pound, and after we finished picking, they'd weigh the buckets and pay us our money. My older brother and I once picked up pecans on the fourths; a fourth of what was picked was our part. When we got finished, there were two coffee sacks full of pecans, and the guy we were working for took three buckets for himself, and then he'd give us one and all the time I'm thinking the three buckets must be for us, but in the end, we only had ten pounds of pecans, and he had the coffee sack almost half full. That's the last time I picked up pecans on the fourths. Most of the time we picked them up, then brought them into town to sell them. Later on, after my father opened his store, he became the pecan man. He bought pecans for fifty cents a pound, and when the truck came from Memphis, he loaded them onto the truck and got sixty-five cents a pound for them. My father was a capitalist—he knew how to make a dollar!

My father passed in 1983, and after I finished my master's degree, I came home from Virginia and started running the family business. By then, educational opportunities had become much better. A lot of people in my age group, and even younger, were going to college. Mississippi really poured money into the local colleges, but I don't think it was done so much to help poor folks, as it was done to keep blacks from being a bigger part of Ole Miss and Mississippi State. I believe that's why they began to make the local schools more inviting.

There were no opportunities here for the young people—it was what we called "lay by time" on the farm. Affirmative action programs from several states were aggressively recruiting good students out of Mississippi high schools, and

*"Today's young people can do anything they want to do.
They just need some guidance, someone to believe in them,
and they must be willing to work for it!"*

Uptown Brown's Sign

we were losing a lot of good black boys. That's changed a lot now, partly because of the casinos and partly because people want to get an education so they can get off government assistance.

That's why we started the Boys to Men Program in February. We wanted to make the younger generation fully aware of what was available to them here in the Delta. We didn't want them buying into the idea that the white man was their biggest enemy. We wanted them to understand that they could be their own biggest enemy; we teach them never to buy into that idea. If they don't, they can control their own lives, and they can be anything they want to be. That's why I'm truly excited about this program, because it allows us to raise young people to another level, where they can live better and achieve more if they'll only reach out there and get it! That's what I told my son, and now he's a second-year med student at Michigan State. Young people can do anything they want to do, if they are just willing to work for it!

Arlyn Holdeman

Mennonite Catfish Farmer • Sunflower

I'm a Mennonite. Most Mennonites came to the United States in the late 1700s and early 1800s. Some came from Switzerland, some came from Germany, some had a Dutch background, and some even came from Russia. My people, the Holdemans, all came from Switzerland. Over the years, my family migrated from Pennsylvania to Ohio and then, finally, to Kansas, where my uncle, Aden Holdeman, founded Heston Manufacturing. He made farm implements, primarily haying equipment. The first Mennonites who actually moved into Mississippi came here to get into the land-leveling business. Some of our folks lived in McAllen, Texas, where the Reynolds brothers were building dirt-moving scrapers, and they told Ivan Koehn, "Why don't you move to the Delta and level land?"

In 1962, when the Koehns moved to Indianola, they were the first Mennonite family in Sunflower County. When we moved here in 1965, we were about the tenth. At one time, I think there were probably sixty or seventy families in the Delta. We've prospered, financially and spiritually.

We're not a big church; we probably just number about twenty thousand total, although we have churches in most of the states, Canada, and Mexico. We serve as an outreach to those around us that feel like they want the true faith, and we try to live as close to the Bible as we can and not be radical. Some people say we live like they believe. I don't know about that, but I do know we just try to live the truth. We don't ignore the modern world; we use vehicles, pickup trucks, and tractors, and electric lights and power tools, but we don't have TVs and radios, and all those things. We use local banks for borrowing money, but we have our own insurance companies. Only we don't call it insurance. We call it an aid plan, because it's a nonprofit organization. We pay a fee, depending on age; everybody just pitches in to one big pot and that pretty much takes care of everything like hospitalization and car insurance. We're not into it for profit. We strictly do it to try and help each other. And we try to help our neighbors. All of that's worked out very well for us. I think we've been quite well accepted in the community. We even have our own school.

Most of our people go through the eighth to the tenth grade, depending on the state requirements. After they get out of school, they go into an apprenticeship program with somebody. They grow up learning to work, working with their dads, and by the time they get out of school, they're on their way. I mean, they can just about do what their dads do, and almost all of them can do carpentry work.

"We feel like we've got something to offer people who are searching for the truth, and we try to provide it for them whether they are white or black, or rich or poor. Our faith has seen us through."

We have a lot of carpenters! We also have lots of land levelers, and we have a good number of farmers. We're not into farming as heavy here as some places are, but land leveling is real big around here and so is the catfish business. I manage 53 catfish ponds on 680 acres. That may seem like a lot, but I've got a neighbor who is not a Mennonite, and he manages 6,000 acres.

Most Mennonites don't work for other people the way I do, but it has always worked for me. I manage this farm for some folks in Switzerland. They're not Mennonites either. They're just doing it for an investment. One of the partners, a doctor in Aberdeen, Mississippi, just became a U.S. citizen. My brother did some dirt work for him in Texas, and when he found out I was in the catfish business, he looked me up. That was in 1985. I was managing another catfish farm in Sunflower when he showed up and asked me if I'd manage this place. He told me we'd build ponds and the shop and whatever else we needed. So I quit working at the other place, and I've been working here ever since. In a couple of years we'll be farming about a thousand acres of catfish. We've done quite well. But we've had some hard times, too.

My wife wound up with cancer, and I've had two sons die. When my oldest son was twelve, he had lymphoma, and they treated him at St. Jude's Hospital in Memphis. But it didn't do any good. He was only twelve years old when he died. My other son—actually, he was my foster son—was eight years old when he died. We had raised our family, and we were still pretty young, so we took in two little boys to raise that didn't have a home, and his older brother backed over him with a pickup. It was a freak accident. They were fishing, and the little boy jumped out of the pickup. He said it was his turn to catch fish, and he went and got the rod and reel out of the back of the pickup. He started fishing, and his brother looked back to see where he was at and took his foot off the brake, and he thought he had the thing in park. It must have been in reverse, and he went to hit the brake—best we could tell, he hit the accelerator. Didn't spin or anything, but he backed right over him. It just curled him up in a ball and the frame of the pickup set right down on top of him. The front wheel fell in a muskrat hole—the only hole around there—so he couldn't move it off of him.

I was right there feeding catfish, but I didn't realize what was going on until I finally just saw water squirting up in the air; he was spinning the tires trying to get the truck off his brother. I ran over there with the feed truck, and he came running down the levee screaming, "I've killed Aaron! I've killed Aaron!" I ran over there to see where he was, but I couldn't find him. "Ryan, where's Aaron?" I asked. "He's in there," he said, pointing at the pond. I jumped in the pond and looked under the pickup, and then I could see him. By the time I got everything sorted out and the truck off of him, he had suffocated. It was tough. But Ryan seems to have gotten over it. He's twenty now, living with his sisters in Okolona. Things are better now for all of us, and I guess we'll just stick with what we're doing.

I suppose we'll finish up farming catfish. We've thought about doing other things, particularly after the boys died and my wife got sick. Then we decided there was no sense in second-guessing the good Lord. So we decided to stay right here and keep our hearts right with the Lord. We try to witness to people by living a good life. We feel like we've got something to offer people who are searching for the truth, and we try to provide it for them whether they are white or black or rich or poor. Our faith has seen us through.

Catfish Ponds
Humphreys County

Dr. Clyde Edward Glenn

Psychiatrist • Parchman Farm
Minister • Chapel Hill Missionary Baptist Church

My father's name was William Glenn. My mother was Essie Glenn. Prior to moving to Cleveland, Mississippi, my parents were sharecroppers in the Heel, a part of the state in the Starkville–Columbus area. After they moved to Cleveland, they purchased a house, and my father became a carpenter, a trade he followed the rest of his life, and my mother did domestic work. In the 1960s, she worked for the Head Start program, and she stayed there until she retired. I am the tenth of eleven children. I have seven brothers and three sisters. My parents never pressured us, they were just supportive; they were great encouragers of whatever pursuits we chose, even though they were not educated themselves. Cleveland, where I grew up, is a town that's sort of a typical southern town. It was divided by the usual physical barrier of the railroad tracks separating the African American community from the Caucasian community. Over the years, there was some bleeding over, but even today, it remains pretty well divided by the railroad track.

I was the first in my family to actually go to a predominantly white junior high school. I started seventh grade at Margaret Green Junior High in the mid to late 1970s. The school had already been integrated. In fact, when I started to school there, I was really somewhat surprised at the number of blacks that were actually there. Most of them were bussed in from Renova and a few other places. Although there were some racial tensions that cropped up from time to time, I got along fairly well with most of the kids, and I didn't have any major problems with my teachers or the staff. Any problems that occurred tended to be more incident-driven than they were a constant, overt, systematic racial tension. Every now and then something would happen, and it would be an issue for a while, but we always managed to work it out. I had the opportunity to choose which school to attend, and the choice I made was a really good one for me, particularly in the quality of the music program they had in the white schools.

I have always loved music. From the time I was about four years old, through my Margaret Green Junior High days, and on into senior high at Cleveland High School, I was a fairly good drummer. After I had some formal training in music, I started focusing specifically on percussion instruments, especially drums. When I graduated from Cleveland High, I received a percussion scholarship to go to Alcorn State University. There I was involved with all the bands. I didn't really have a choice. I had a scholarship, so I had to play in concert, marching, and jazz

"We decided it was important to raise our kids around an extended family."

band. When they needed a drummer, they called me. It actually all worked to my benefit; I had to study a little harder and be a little bit more disciplined, but being in band did teach me discipline, and it forced me to mature. Although I was just an average student in high school, I excelled academically as an undergraduate, where I finished with a biology, pre-medicine degree.

I did my graduate work at the University of Iowa College of Medicine, where I received my M.D. degree. I decided my junior year that what attracted me most of the varied specialties was psychiatry. I found the patients to be much more intriguing, and they didn't really fit into a classical mold like other patients in the sense that you never really knew what you were going to get on any given day. That intrigued me; both the illnesses themselves and the challenges the patients had to overcome that were associated with their mental illness.

During this time, I also noticed that a number of African Americans were frequently misdiagnosed for cultural reasons. For instance, an African American might have symptoms that would mean one thing if it were an Anglo, and something totally different to an African American. In my own small way, when I could, I wanted to identify and correct those discrepancies. The fact that there are very few African Americans who actually go into psychiatry also drew me to the field. I thought I would be in a unique position to render services to African Americans who were mentally ill. This also allowed my colleagues to gain from my insights into the African American community.

I went to Ohio State University for my residency, and I had a great learning experience there. I really felt as though I was adequately prepared for the challenges that I would face in my practice. My wife is also a physician, and we met our first year in medical school. She is not a psychiatrist; she's a pathologist. After we married, she finished her three-year military obligation, and it was at that time that we decided to move south.

Our decision was based on many factors; my parents were only thirty miles away and we had an entire network of brothers, sisters, and cousins and we decided it was important to raise our kids around an extended family. Things also worked out for us professionally in Clarksdale. I was hired by Charter Behavioral Health Services, a private provider, and she went to work at Northwest Mississippi Regional Medical Center, a top-notch local hospital. In June 2000, I picked up Charter's contract with Parchman Prison, and I've been there ever since.

This prison population is a bit different in the sense that it's overwhelmingly African American. The patients deal with lots of alcohol and drug abuse, in addition to any other psychiatric problems that they might have. As I said, it is a very difficult population to work with, because while I talk about that biological, psychological, and social approach, to a great extent what we end up doing in the prison setting is really just treating them from the biological end because I can't do very much about their social environment. In fact, in many cases, the social environment within the prison is what brought about the psychiatric problems to begin with. There are lots of issues that I have to work through in order to get treatment for my patients. Then, after I figure out a treatment protocol, we may not even be able to afford it because our resources are so limited.

It's unfortunate that the state of Mississippi has adopted a punishment and incarceration approach, instead of a prevention and treatment approach, which would be much cheaper in the long run. African Americans, however, tend to be victimized by the letter of the law, rather than the spirit of the law.

In Mississippi, I think there's a much greater likelihood that the first-time African American offender will actually go to jail or prison, as opposed to the first-time white offender. I say this because I see ten or twelve African Americans in my practice for every white person, so there's quite a discrepancy, and I believe it can be traced to one drug law. Basically, crack cocaine, which is much more popular in the African American community, will get the offender fifteen years for a "five-dollar rock." When compared to the use of crystal meth in the white community, some of these white kids are getting as little as thirteen months in jail and sometimes even probation. I did raise some significant concerns about that issue with a few of our elected officials, and what I saw eventually happen was that there was much more truth-in-sentencing now than there used to be. That is my approach. I tend to be willing to work within the system to facilitate change.

But one thing that I am very much opposed to is always hiding behind being victimized by society. Some, but not all of our problems, are caused by racism. However, I don't see any white men coming into our neighborhoods, shooting up our boys. We're doing that to ourselves. And I don't see any of them standing on the corner selling crack. We're doing that to ourselves. It is our responsibility to change the things going on in our neighborhoods. I don't want to minimize the effect that racism, classism, and all the other isms have had along the line. I certainly don't want to minimize that, but what I'm saying is that it's not the only factor. I believe there are things that I can do individually in regards to changing certain behavioral patterns that will make a positive difference in my family, my neighborhood, and the larger community. That is why I went into the ministry.

One of the local churches, Chapel Hill Missionary Baptist Church, interviewed me, and after having been without a pastor for six months, they called me as their pastor; the fourth Sunday of April will be my fifth anniversary. I try and minister to the whole person. My conceptualization of the ministry is that we, the church, are actually an extension of the ministry of Christ. It started with Him. He institutes the church to carry out and to carry forth his mandates into the world, to allow people to experience him, to encounter him, and that's done through His church. It is my responsibility as a pastor to always keep that vision out in front of the people and to frequently remind people that this is our calling. That's what we are supposed to do. In the context of that, however, I see it sort of extended beyond just Sunday morning services. I want to help people live better, more fulfilling lives. That's what we are seeking to do through our many, diverse church ministries.

On Fridays, during the tax season, people in the community can come to our church and have their taxes done free of charge. Another ministry, which started just yesterday, is an annual abstinence seminar, where our goal is to inform our youth about their bodies, because the teen pregnancy rate in Coahoma County is so high. We are very frank and very open with them. We teach them anatomy, we teach them the physiology that is involved, and we try to help them understand that while God has created us as sexual beings, and our sexuality is something that we should cherish, it still brings with it responsibilities. So, in that sense, we hope to make something of a difference by teaching and educating our youth so that we can somehow curb this problem that just overwhelmingly plagues this area. My challenge, which is not an easy one, is to create programs for the church that affirm who we are—as Christians, African Americans, and as ordinary people.

David R. Hargett

Superintendent • East Tallahatchie County Schools • Charleston

I grew up in a poor, hard-working family. My father, Flynn Hargett, was from Red Bay, Alabama. In 1927, when he was twenty-seven, he came to Tallahatchie County to work in the timber business; he cut hardwood—oak and poplar—for the Belmont Lumber Company. The county was big then—thirty thousand people. That same year, the year of the big flood, he married my mother, Frankie Mae Champion. My father and mother had nine children, five boys and four girls; I was number seven. I had two younger brothers. I was born on Teasdale Road, two miles north of Charleston, where my father had opened a little country store. When I was born, in October 1945, most of our neighbors were poor, like us. But even though we were poor, we always had plenty of food, and we always had plenty of fun! We all worked hard, too, and after all the work was done we sat on the porch and listened to the stories that my father, mother, and grandfather told. Our tradition was to pass on stories, but that was hard for me because I grew up with a speech impediment.

I couldn't talk too well, and I struggled; I repeated my first three years of school. But something amazing happened when I got into Miss Lilly Adams's fourth-grade class. I never will forget the help, encouragement, and love she gave me. I learned from her that teachers do make a difference. I found out she had a daughter who was totally deaf. I think that's one reason Miss Adams took an interest in helping me, because she knew I was struggling. But in the 1950s, Tallahatchie County didn't offer special services, so Miss Adams arranged to bring in a speech therapist from outside the county. He helped me and several other students in the class. I guess you could say I was a late bloomer. I made up several years of school, and after I graduated in 1966, I went to Northwest Community College.

During my two years at Northwest I had three jobs. I served meals in the recreation center, worked as a dorm monitor, and as my third job, I worked across the street at Krum Kraft Furniture. For a poor country boy, I was doing pretty good! I was making money and going to school, too. After my first two years I had to stop school for eighteen months to earn some money, but eventually I graduated from Delta State University.

John Alderman gave me my first job in education; I taught seventh- and eighth-grade history and science. Although I liked teaching, after two years in the classroom, I realized I really wanted to be in administration, so I went back

"Even though we were poor, we had plenty of food and plenty of fun!"

**St. Joseph's
Football Practice
Greenville**

to school and got my master's degree. After serving as the assistant principal and principal of the middle school, I eventually ran for superintendent of schools.

My job used to be an elected office. The first time I ran, in 1983, I lost, but the second time I ran, in 1987, I won. It was a somewhat hollow victory: the school system was a million dollars in debt, and we were on level 1 probation, the lowest level. But we eventually sold a few oil and gas leases, had a couple of timber sales, and we were blessed with a few private donors. Now, nearly twenty years later, we are two million dollars in the black, and the school is at level 4, the best!

Our extended school program has helped a lot. Not only has it helped the parents, but our test scores have gone up. Our kids, who are 60 percent African American and 40 percent white, scored higher last year than the students at the private academies. An expanded preschool program would help even more, but we can only serve kindergarten kids, starting at age five. We can serve three or four year olds with speech therapy, but only if the child is ruled developmentally delayed. I'm proud of our kids, and I'm proud of our system.

I am married to Carol Williams Hargett, and we have one daughter, Candace, who went to school here; she was valedictorian, got a 30 on her ACT, and graduated from the University of Mississippi Law School. I attribute my success to God and my mother; she took all us kids to church, and that kept us all out of trouble.

David R. Hargett

Dr. Patricia Johnson

Doctor of Chiropractic Medicine
Cofounder Sunflower River Blues Association
Former Co-owner of Stackhouse & Rooster Blues Records • Clarksdale

I moved to the Delta about twenty years ago. I'm a practicing chiropractor, but I also was drawn here because of my interest in the blues. I had a small booking agency in California, and I was consulting on film projects. I came here and just really fell in love with the place. There were so many blues musicians who were still here, and I was delighted to see and hear them on their own turf. A blues resurgence was just starting, and most of the musicians were just playing in the local clubs and juke joints. My partner, Jim O'Neal, the founder of *Living Blues* magazine and Rooster Blues Records, and I made it a point to seek out the musicians who were here and to document what was going on. We did this by producing many recordings of local blues musicians. We also wanted to support what we saw as a resurgence of the blues, so we worked with the local chamber of commerce, trying to help them understand that Clarksdale tourism was a major potential industry and that people would be coming here whether we developed it or not, because the Delta had more or less become a blues mecca.

Clarksdale may not be the birthplace of the blues, but it certainly is the cradle of the blues. Historically, this place was a stopping point for musicians around the Delta—a stopping point on the way to Memphis, on the way to St. Louis, on the way to Chicago, and to other cities where many of the well-known bluesmen and women made their marks. Many musicians came from here. We started educating the general public, and that stirred up a lot of local interest. We also documented and recorded as many of the musicians as we could. Rooster was a small, independent record company, but well known and respected in the industry. We founded the Stackhouse, a local arts, gifts, and music store, and it became a sort of a clearing house for blues information. At the time, the Blues Museum was very small, and it was not even staffed. Sid Graves, director of the Carnegie Public Library, founded it in 1979.

What stirred up a lot of national interest was when several film companies started shooting documentaries. The major networks, CNN, Mississippi Public Television, and films like *Deep Blues,* utilized local talent to tell their stories. The BBC filmed *The Promised Land* and National Geographic filmed a special called *The Blues Highway* that was nominated for an Academy Award. They did a lot of wonderful local interviews, but the musicians, more often than not, were a little

*"There are people around here who really don't care one way
or another about the blues, but they recognize that the Sunflower River
Blues Festival is an institution that's shining a light
on Clarksdale, a very positive light!"*

bit shy about talking about their music. They played, and they enjoyed it, but for a period of time the blues had been underground; grandpa played it, maybe grandma, or aunts and uncles, and they weren't used to so much attention. They knew the music, and they played at home, and when they started coming out, it was exciting, but only a handful of local musicians who were on the juke joint circuit were playing regularly: Frank Frost, Sam Carr, Big Jack Johnson, and the Wesley Jefferson Band. In addition, the "Chitlin Circuit" featured artists like Bobby Rush, Little Milton, and Bobby Bland. They were all playing publicly, and they were pretty active locally, but people weren't significantly promoting their music. As a result, even though there was a lot more music around, the musicians who played in the Delta were, for the most part, still working their day jobs.

About that time, as national interest grew, one of the things that Jim and I were both very adamant about was protecting the integrity of the music and the people. A part of the history of the blues is blues musicians being ripped off, and we were staunch fighters against that happening. As interest in the Delta increased, there were numerous film crews and writers who came here with their own agendas. They tried to use this area to prove stereotypes, and most of us were very quick to not let them get away with that kind of behavior.

Unfortunately, it was somewhat easy to take advantage of the musicians because very, very few were making a living playing the blues. The economics of it are such that those who are making a solid living, like Big Jack Johnson and Lonnie Shields, had to leave Mississippi in order to be on the club circuit. Now they play at a lot of different, better-paying venues, instead of making a little bit of pocket change at home on the weekends. So we lose a little something when quality musicians leave, but certainly, for them, they're getting out there, and they're able to make a living. And, of course, Big Jack will be coming home for the festival, which is wonderful. He's always a big hit.

Most of the juke joints have closed down. Some clubs here, while they do have music, aren't really juke joints. Those places were developed to cater to the tourists, but that has its good side. People have a place to go where they can feel comfortable, and there is also good local support—not huge, but enough to keep things moving on the weekends. That's when most of the local musicians play because they work during the week.

The Sunflower River Blues Festival actually grew out of what was a Downtown Merchants Association's event—Downtown Days. The merchants all got together and had a combination street sale and outdoor affair designed to support local businesses. While still in California, I helped them book some of the performers. For instance, I booked Little Milton to come and perform. 1988 was the first year we really kicked it off and actually called it a festival. The Downtown Merchants Association, Clarksdale Chamber of Commerce, and Mississippi Delta Arts Council all cosponsored the event. The first festival was lovely. It was small, and we weren't able to sell beer, now a financial boone, but it was very warm and well received. It was held on the riverbank the first year, and we named the festival the Sunflower Riverbank Blues Festival.

We changed the name to Sunflower River Blues Festival two years later when we moved downtown to the old freight depot. We had two stages, one for bands and one acoustic. It was marvelous! That was also when we made our first big mistake. We provided free music during the day, and when we tried to move everyone into the Thompson Center for a paid show, it didn't work. When you give free blues away all day long, and people get filled up with that wonderful entertainment, then it's hard to get them to pay for it that night!

The next year we had to change gears very quickly because our backers pulled out two weeks before the festival. We literally flooded the whole area with pleas for help, and I think we rounded up about $750. The festival was held at Martin Luther King Park, which is a beautiful park. We told the musicians that we didn't have a lot of money, but that we would split it between all of them. We had a little booth where we sold Coke, and the chamber of commerce sold lemonade. We had one vendor, Boss Hog, and he was wonderful. It turned out to be very nice.

We used a cotton trailer for the stage, and Johnnie Billington, a local musician, brought some sound equipment. We pulled it off, and we had visitors from all over the world. That was when we decided we needed to be more organized, and we started getting a group of people together and founded the Sunflower River Blues Association. It was incorporated, and we applied for and received all of our tax-exempt documents. For a few years it was just a handful of volunteers, but then it grew and grew and grew. We started getting grants from the Mississippi Arts Commission, and we attracted more corporate sponsors. Coors, our local distributor, has been with us since the beginning, and they've done everything from bringing out huge tubs of ice to providing trash barrels. It was a real community effort, and it has grown every year. Since then, things have changed a lot.

The Delta Blues Museum is now located in the old freight depot, and it annually attracts

Poster of Sunflower River Blues & Gospel Festival

thousands of tourists to Clarksdale. New businesses are thriving, like the Ground Zero Blues Club and Madidi Restaurant, co-owned by award-winning actor Morgan Freeman, Attorney Bill Luckett and former Sunflower River Blues Association Chairman Howard Stovall, and they draw many visitors to Clarksdale, offering good food and regular live music.

Many of the musicians around this area, including Big Jack Johnson (who has returned home but still travels extensively), are making a living practicing their craft for larger local audiences. Juke joints such as Red's, Sarah's Kitchen, and Messenger's (open since the 1940s) are other places visitors can find live music fairly often. Information about local venues can be found on the Cathead website. Cathead Blues and Folk Art, Inc. is a record, folk and blues store on Delta Avenue—much like the long closed Stackhouse—in its heyday! There are people around here who really don't care one way or another about blues, but they do recognize that this is an institution that's shining a light on Clarksdale, a very positive light!

Chafik Chamoun

Restaurant Owner • Clarksdale

My wife and I came here in 1954, from Sarhian, a little village in Lebanon's Bekah Valley. My family in Lebanon was not rich, but they were not poor either. I would say they were middle class. They farmed and sold what they raised in one of several little grocery stores they owned, along with things like tobacco, soft drinks, sugar, and coffee. I was going to school in the village, and my grandfather, my mother's father, sent me money regularly to help me out, and I worked at the grocery store. I quickly figured out that I wasn't going to get rich working at the grocery store, so that's when my wife and I moved to America. I had an uncle who lived in Clarksdale, and he used to have a grocery store. After about a month, when I couldn't find work, he put me to work in the store.

My boss was an Italian, a good Christian fellow. He tried to help me, but I couldn't speak the language, and I didn't know anything, so he put me to work taking black eyed peas out of a bushel basket and putting them in plastic bags to sell to the customers one bag at a time. You always hear that you get money out of the trees in the United States, but when I came here, I found out it was a whole lot different. I discovered you could make money, but you had to work hard. I was working ten hours a day, seven days a week. Seventy hours for twenty dollars. My wife was so unhappy about my hours, I actually thought I was going to have to leave and return to Lebanon

Finally, one day the Italian grocer said, "You are not happy here, are you?"

"No I am not," I replied.

He said, "Your people have always done well taking merchandise to the country. If I were in your place I would go ahead and try."

I agreed, and the second day I told my grandmother I wanted a suitcase, so she went to the attic and got a metal suitcase that must have weighed twenty pounds.

Then I realized I didn't have anything to sell. My grandfather told a local store to let me have forty dollars' worth of merchandise on credit. So I went to the store and bought a dozen ladies' stockings and some women's underwear. Then I put them in the suitcase and went to work. It was only a five-minute walk to the black section of town, and pretty soon I was knocking on doors and talking to potential customers. They asked me about the size, and I didn't know what size it was. They either gave me a dollar or they owed me a dollar or two. About two or three months later, my wife read in the paper that Rawleigh Products was

"Most of them didn't know how to pronounce my name,
so I just told them I was the Rawleigh man."

looking for a sales representative in this area. Rawleigh sold home products, like Watkins.

I went with the sales representative to Memphis, and he took me to Riverside, where the company was located. I bought three hundred dollars' worth of goods on credit. My uncle had to sign for it. And I went and bought a six-hundred-dollar Plymouth and put the merchandise in the trunk. Then I realized I had everything I needed, but I didn't know what in the hell I was selling!

The company gave me two slips; one for retail and one for wholesale. The wholesale slip was white, and the other one was blue. People knew about the merchandise, and they were always glad to see me coming, but when I started I always met the planters first. They were always real friendly, and they never told me to leave. In fact, they never looked down on me because of my language, or my skin color, or where I came from.

"You go ahead," they'd say. "You look like a poor boy trying to make a living. Just don't bother the workers while they're working." One of them even said, "I have a store and you're selling stuff like we have at the store, but you look like you just got to this country and you're trying to make a living, You go ahead and don't worry about it." He even took me and introduced me to his people.

Even after he introduced me most of them didn't know how to pronounce my name, so I just told them I was the Rawleigh man. I sold fly spray, garden dust, roach killer, rat poison, soap, perfume, deodorant, cold medicine, and liniment, things people needed. They'd come to the trunk and point. "That's what I want," they'd say. Quite often I couldn't tell them how much the goods cost. "What does it say here?" I'd say, looking at the blue slip. And they'd look at it and say, "$2.25." I'd say, "OK" and so they bought it, and my business prospered. Sometimes I even gave out a little credit.

My customers were 100 percent black, and I can tell you from personal experience that they don't come any nicer. I used to make most of my collections this time of year from eleven until two, that's when they weren't working. Then I would go home and about five o'clock I would go back and see the rest. It was all collections; first they'd buy and then I'd collect. That's how I did business. I usually started collections about eleven o'clock and went until about two o'clock. If it was too far to go home, about two thirty I would lay down under a tree and take a nap until it was time to start back collecting about five. I had a little Willis jeep, and I used to pray that I would have a place to park the Jeep and not have to worry about how hot it was.

I stayed on the Rawleigh route about thirty years. By the time I was finished I had twelve routes. I did that besides doing something else. I worked for Tallahatchie Equipment Company, about thirty-five miles away. This time of year it was nothing for me to sell forty or fifty gallons of fly spray. After I started going from house to house, when I finished that route I'd wait two weeks before I'd run the same route again, but in the early 1970s, when I stopped selling Rawleigh

Products, I closed all twelve routes. I really miss my customers. Of course, most of them have died by now, and then the new apartments came, and then Wal-Mart came, so the country just faded away. You can't even find a house in the country now. The only thing left are apartments, and they are not a good place to go sell things. But we eventually found a grocery store inside the city limits, and we bought the grocery store and stayed in the grocery business for several years. In 1972, in addition to running the grocery store, I started selling cars. I sold cars for twelve years, then I get tired of the car business, and I sold shoes for a little while, until this restaurant came up for sale in 1990. Things have gone all right since then, and I don't regret the direction my life has taken. Things were booming back then, and the Rawleigh Products business helped me raise my family.

All six of our children were born in this town. My oldest son, Robert, is an attorney, and my second-oldest child, Vivian, is a speech therapist. The third child, Elizabeth, is a doctor's assistant, and the girl working here with me is a licensed dietician. Mona, next to the youngest, has a degree in hotel and restaurant management, and my youngest son lives in Conway, Arkansas. He's an electrical engineer, and he works with an energy company. All of them went to college and all of them graduated. For me and my kids the American dream really did come true. People complain about the United States, but I say let them go overseas! At five o'clock in the morning people are lined up at the American embassy, trying to get the necessary paperwork to come here. I can assure you that the whole world would swap places with us. They might not get to be a millionaire, but if you come here, work hard, and are honest, then if you don't make it there is something wrong.

Reverend M. C. Johnson

Director of Missions • North Delta Baptist Association • Clarksdale

When they asked us to assume the role of missions director in Clarksdale, I told them I didn't have a background in social ministries, but if I took it we'd just have to make mistakes together, and that's what we've done. We've tried a lot of things that haven't worked, but, praise God, there's a lot of things we've tried that have worked. I love to work with the pastors, do administrative work, and coordinate the twenty-seven churches in our association. I work with Tunica, Quitman, and Coahoma counties. Of the twenty-seven churches and one mission, twenty-five of those are black congregations, which was unheard of in the Delta until about twelve years ago. We have come a long way as far as race goes. I have a good rapport with all the black ministers, and I'm frequently invited to speak in their churches.

In our office in Clarksdale, where we have what we call a crisis ministry, we help about three thousand families a year with food, or clothing, or furniture and house repair, or maybe winterization or medical expenses. We also have a number of people who are certified to teach literacy, and they do it voluntarily, and we hold a lot of health fairs, mission revivals, vacation Bible schools, and backyard Bible clubs. We even do sports clinics—anything that we can do to reach people for the Lord, and to help them have a better life. We got into home repair several years ago, and if people will provide the money for the materials, we will get a team to come in and repair their homes. Of course we have to be discretionary about this because we're not going to repair a man's home who can afford to have it repaired.

We also don't get into new construction, but we have repaired twelve or thirteen churches, and two of them had to be almost completely rebuilt. We go to Arizona every February to help build a new church. We've made twenty-one trips out there. In May, we go south to McAllen, Texas, and we'll be taking about eighty houses that have been cut out and color-coded to make it easy to put them together. In July, the youth from our area and several other areas will go down to Mexico, where our youth will erect houses under the supervision of adults. In June we always have a group that goes to the Honduras. We had a Singspiration Friday night and raised $4,500 to help on that project. Groups also come here to work. This year we'll have about twenty teams that will come in from eight different states. The World Changers have come here twice, and we have a group coming in next summer called Missions Mobilization. They're bringing a couple of hundred people in, over a period of two weeks, to help do home repairs. When

"We help about three thousand families a year with food, or clothing, or furniture and house repair; or maybe winterization or medical expenses."

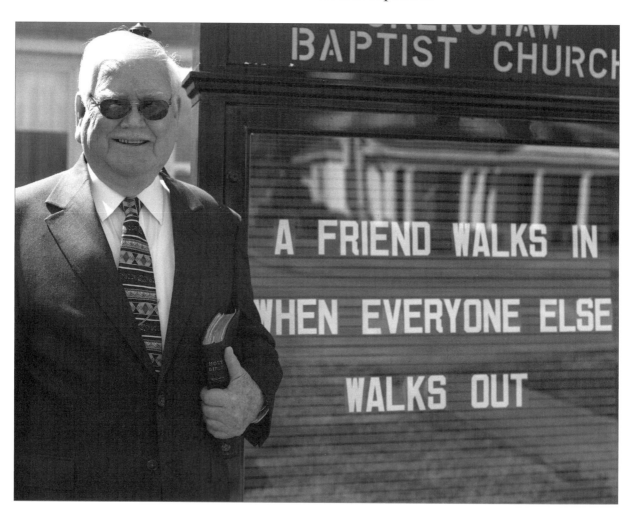

I say home repairs, I mean a new roof, or painting, or fixing the windows, or repairing the floor, or rebuilding the porch.

In addition to the building programs, we also operate a crisis pregnancy center, where we see about seventy young ladies a month. We have twenty-five ladies that are volunteer counselors. The young women come in and we provide a pregnancy test which they take themselves because we are not a medical facility. Then, if they aren't pregnant, we counsel them about abstinence, and if they are pregnant, we give them a baby bag and enroll them in Bible study. Each time they come to Bible study, they can get a new item in that baby bag, and over a period of eight or nine months, they'll get everything they need to take care of a young baby. We also provide the ladies with maternity clothes and things of that nature. We have some doctors who provide prenatal care for free if the young women don't have any money. We've been very fortunate in that area. All these services are for poor people.

We have a very active ministry at Friars Point, a predominantly black town. We recently bought an old schoolhouse over there, and this fall we'll be teaching literacy classes, starting a senior adult program, and starting a day care. We've already got ballfields to keep the youth off the streets, and we'll also be starting a senior adult feeding program. We're getting state certification for that now. But we don't just work with the African American community. I thank God we can work with people of all races, like Hispanic people. The Hispanic population in Mississippi is growing so fast. By 2020, 40 percent of the people in the United States will be Hispanic. Next Saturday we are going to have a Hispanic pastor come in from Batesville, and he'll be showing us how to get cell groups started. We start in a home with one person, and they bring in their friends, then so on. Hopefully, we can get a Hispanic church going.

We also have a lot of Chinese people in Clarksdale. They're some of the finest people you'll meet anywhere. We have three Chinese deacons in our church, and we're hoping to start a Chinese service as soon as we can find a Chinese pastor. We haven't been able to come up with anyone yet. We are involved in a lot of things, and as far as the future goes, we'll just keep improving housing and teaching literacy classes. Fortunately, we don't have to do it all alone.

Pete Johnson, who heads up the North Delta Regional Development Council, is making a tremendous impact in creating infrastructure. Of course, when you look at Pete, he's got Mississippi, Arkansas, Missouri, and Tennessee to look after, so he's spread real thin. He works in the Delta, as well as all of those states. He's a Godly man, and I think he's doing a great job. Another one doing a great job is Senator Delma Furniss, but he's not going to run again. He's retiring, and he's going to be missed. I suppose you could say he's the man responsible for making Highway 61 four lanes into the Delta, and they're naming the new rest area on Highway 49 and Highway 61 after him. He's had a great influence in bringing things to the Delta that are going to help here. But the Delta is full of uneducated people, as well as poor housing, poor health facilities, and the highest teenage pregnancy rate in Mississippi. Of the three counties that I serve, two school systems are on probation, and the third, Tunica County, has been taken over by the state.

When I came to the Delta-Greenwood area about twenty-eight years ago, it was pathetic. Our black friends were held down, jobwise, socially, and in lots of other ways. I've always been amazed how someone can look down on anyone. I was raised in Louisiana, and I never understood racism as a boy, or as a grown man either. That was then. Now you see black people in leadership roles. Andrew Thompson, the sheriff of Coahoma County, is one of the finest sheriffs that you will find anywhere. Andrew is a black man, and he's just as fair as he can be. And we also have a black mayor, Henry Espy. And there are numerous other black people in key leadership positions. It's a good thing because the old plantation mentality we had here demanded that they stay behind a mule and a plow, but things have sure changed, and that change has definitely been for the better.

Far from Home
Greenville Cemetery

Voices of the Delta

Chuck Miller

Former General Manager • Grand Casino • Tunica

I got into the gaming industry purely by accident. I was pursuing a degree in medicine when I enlisted in the U.S. Army in 1968. I did a tour of duty in Vietnam, and when I came back I enrolled in medical science refresher courses at the University of Nevada, Las Vegas. At the time I was also trying to get into the Children's Hospital in Los Angeles, but I was trying to support myself working as a hospital orderly, which didn't pay very well. A friend of mine suggested that I work the night shift at a casino, and I could go to school during the day. I went to dealing school and learned how to deal craps, and as they say the rest is history. That was in 1972. For the next twenty years, I worked at Union Plaza in downtown Las Vegas, on the Vegas Strip, at Lake Tahoe, and in Reno. I did it all: I was a dealer, I worked in food service, I was a valet, swept floors as a casino porter, carried change and worked as an attendant in slots, worked in the restaurant pits cleaning and washing dishes, I learned cash/credit operations, made beds, and even cleaned bathrooms. I learned something about just about every part of casino/hotel operations, and in 1983 I got into management.

I went from operations to marketing, and I stayed in marketing until 1992. That was the year I joined this company. My first two years with the company were as the regional vice president of marketing for the Gulfport/Biloxi properties. In 1994, I went to the Grand Casino in Coushatta, Louisiana, as the general manager. I came to Grand Casino Tunica as executive vice president and general manager about a year ago. Tunica has been in operation for about five years, and there is a real interesting story that goes along with this place.

In order for a casino to be legal in Mississippi, it is supposed to be on a boat-type structure, so it actually has to float. It's supposed to be close to natural water. We're very close to the Mississippi River in a tributary called Buck Lake. It's directly fed by the Mississippi. We float in about four feet of water, although most of the support facilities, like hotels and receiving docks, are on land. Anything that has something to do with a gaming device has to float.

In Tunica, gaming is an emerging industry. That means they have never had it here before, so some people are for it and some are against. I don't think the acceptance is that broad yet, but what opponents are beginning to find out is this industry is not going to go away. It has a great deal of credibility, and at the same time, it has a huge benefit to the local population. In the early 1970s, when I joined this industry, it was probably selling a dream; gambling is likened to selling a dream.

"Within two years Tunica will become a billion-dollar-a-year gaming market."

We're in the gaming industry, but we're also in the entertainment industry. We're giving people quality for the dollars that they spend in terms of entertainment and service. Those are the two products that we sell—gaming and entertainment. At the same time, bear in mind that you can come in here and catch live entertainment, and eat some of the best food ever for great prices. You can literally come to this property, never gamble, and still have a great time. But we also do a lot of gaming. According to the Mississippi Gaming Commission, this market is the third-largest gaming market in the country. We are behind Las Vegas and Atlantic City, and our goal is to someday be second. I don't think there's any way that we can ever catch Las Vegas, but our analyst tells us that within two years Tunica will become a billion-dollar-a-year gaming market.

In Tunica, all of these things were desperately needed. Prior to the casinos, I have been told that Tunica County was like a third-world country. There was very high unemployment, and all the problems that go along with extreme poverty, like crime and social problems. They called it Sugar Ditch. I've only been here a year, but in five years the casinos have turned all that around. I will tell you right now that anybody who wants a job, and a pretty decent-paying job at that, can get a job. And anyone who wants the training that they can use to develop opportunities for the future can certainly get the training they need. Many of the minimum-wage jobs earn tips. The average wage on this property is a little over nine dollars an hour. At the same time, our associates earn benefits which they never had before. We provide them with health insurance, dental insurance, on-site day care, we teach GED classes, and we provide our associates with full benefit packages. We also have a tuition reimbursement program, which means if an associate wants to earn further education credits, we'll actually pay for their tuition. We train our dealers in-house, because, up to now, the state educational system has not been geared toward courses that are gaming related. That's just beginning to change, and I'm very glad to see that change occurring.

We contribute a tremendous amount of money to the tax base. Twelve percent of our gross goes to the state. Tunica County gets half-a-percent hotel tax and a half-of-a percent food tax. Believe it or not, there are about 5,000 hotel rooms in this market right now. It's crazy, but somewhere around 1,500–1,600 are just now opening. We think hotel rooms are a key to this market. This is an industry that is too often misunderstood. It's populated by a lot of plain, ordinary folks who are trying to make a living and doing the best job they can. Quite frankly, I think we are doing a very good job.

This is a high-energy job, but what we do have are pockets where it's kind of sedate. A lot of how the staff and our guests react to our environment has a great deal to do with the music we play. We do exit interviews with our customers, and we ask them what they liked and what they didn't like. One of the things we ask them about is the music. It varies from a kind of very light jazz and some classical, to the 1950s and contemporary rock we play in the gaming room, where it is a little higher energy.

We attract a pretty high element on the social scale. I have worked in some casinos, particularly in Reno, that attracted a pretty seedy element. They kind of walk around and try to figure out ways to take advantage of us, but they don't stick around very long when they see our security. Our security staff is very good at their jobs, and they are ever present. You wouldn't believe the technology in the building, and it is all designed to protect our guests, our staff, and our investment. We are not an easy mark, and that's what some of those folks are trying to find. The Grand and the other casinos in Tunica are just simply not conducive to attracting that element. Our demographics show that we attract mostly middle-class folks and above. I'm also on the floor a great deal of the time, and when I'm not there, I know all of our security and surveillance associates are constantly on guard.

Managing twenty-eight-hundred associates is the dream of a lifetime. My best moments are walking the resort and on the casino floor, visiting with our guests and talking with associates. The worst moments are just trying to dig through all the paperwork and keep up with all the local and state regulations. I am fortunate to have a staff that takes care of many of the things that would normally eat up my time. When I'm on the floor, I'm basically socializing, even though I get paid for it. We've got three eight-hour shifts that go on seven days a week, and that does create some problems for me at home. I have a lovely wife and three children, and we have to be dedicated to one another, but they are understanding of the demands placed on a senior executive in the industry. I do spend some graveyard shifts here, and I do spend swing shifts and day shifts, so my hours are quite odd.

I've been in the gaming industry for twenty-five years, so it's natural for me. My wife knew what I did when we got married (she also worked in gaming as a very successful player development host), so the lifestyle we lead didn't come as a surprise to her. The general adage that we in this industry go by is that we work when other folks are off, and we are off when they're working. The weekends are very, very high volume, while Monday, Tuesday, Wednesday, and Thursday are not quite as busy. I spend as much time at home as I can, and occasionally my family will come in here and visit me. We'll have dinner and our children will play at Kids Quest, an entertainment facility on the property just for children. This is a very busy, high-energy business, but it has been very good to me and my family.

Laura Hart Hearn

Retired Schoolteacher • Clarksdale

I was born in 1912 in Yazoo County, and I came here in 1925. I had five sisters and one brother, my father, John, and my mother, Maggie. There were nine of us all together. Now they are all dead. I am the only one still alive. When I started school, I had to walk three miles to school and three miles home, six miles, every day, just to go to a little one-room school. My older sister, Frankie, was a nurse, and she didn't think I should have to walk so far, just to get to school. So when I was in the fifth grade, she came to Yazoo County, brought me to this house, and enrolled me in classes at Myrtle Hall School. It was a black school for students K–12. I went there until I finished high school. I wasn't a particularly good student, but I did the best I could, and I loved that school. The teachers, like Mr. George H. Oliver, were wonderful. I graduated in 1932, and I've been here ever since. I just loved teaching.

When I was a little child, sometimes I'd walk outside, and I'd look up and talk to the Lord. I told Him I wanted to be a classroom teacher. I guess one of the things that made me like that is because of what happened to me on my first day of school. I was so nervous that I cried. I didn't cry out loud. But the teacher heard me and whipped me. It made my sister Frankie so mad that she didn't know what to do. She put her arms around me and told me that everything would be all right.

And I think that was the thing that made me want to be a teacher, because so many teachers don't understand children. And I was one of them that had shouldered the brunt of a teacher's misunderstanding. That was why I wanted to teach and why I loved teaching so much. I lived with my sister until I graduated from high school. During that time my mother passed, and Frankie, the first black registered nurse in Clarksdale, took me completely over. She worked for two white doctors, Dr. Hughes and Dr. Dodd; they turned an old school into a hospital for black patients. Frankie ran the hospital for them, and when they had emergencies or operations, it was all done right there where Frankie worked.

After I graduated from Myrtle Hall School, I went to Alcorn State University for four years. Then I came back home. My sister still maintained this house, but after I had finished college and came back here, she became very sick and passed away. First her husband died, and then she died. They didn't have any children, so when she died, she willed the house and the eighty-acre farm in Yazoo County to me. I was her baby sister. I'm glad she willed it to me because I didn't want to go back to living in the country without electricity or indoor plumbing, and having to fight all the snakes and insects. I have always been a city girl, and I still am.

"All I ever wanted to be was a teacher!"

I majored in home economics in college, and after I finished school, my first teaching assignment was at Winona, Mississippi. I taught home economics because it was the best-paying job for teachers at that time. I stayed there quite a few years. When I started, I was the only single teacher on the faculty. Since I didn't have a family, they gave me the basketball coach's job, for both boys and girls. My boys always outdid their boys, and they'd say, "How can we let a woman do this to us? How can we keep letting her boys beat us?" They got angry, but I just laughed because I thought it was funny. I stayed there three years until a government job opened up in Greenwood. My job was to teach poor people about basic nutrition, cleanliness, and health care. I did that for a couple of years, until I married my college sweetheart, Charles Hearn.

Charles was a big, tall, good-looking man. We met at Alcorn. He also played saxophone in the Alcorn band. I've still got his saxophone, and after both of us finished college, we got married. We had three children—two boys and one girl. He served in World War II, and he got shot nine times by the military police during a race riot when he was stationed in Phoenix, Arizona. There were white and black troops stationed at the fort; the white troops were off during the day, and the black troops were off at night. Somehow or other, the two groups got into a fight. My husband had just left my boarding house, headed back to his barracks, and he walked right into the middle of that fight. By then, the military police had come to break up the fight. They opened fire, and he got shot nine times. He stayed in the hospital for five weeks. I was right there taking care of him. He went to his grave with a bullet in his back.

I wasn't active in the civil rights movement because I just didn't believe in it. Teachers didn't make much money at that time, especially black teachers. That, of course, was when things were segregated. When integration came, that made it a little better for all of us, black and white teachers. But I wasn't for all the marching and the sit-ins and the upheavals. I always believed that if people would get together and talk about their problems, they could be solved. I didn't believe in being so critical about other people because if I was that critical of them, then they'd be that critical of me. God didn't make us all alike. He didn't mean for us all to be alike, and I saw it that way, although I got along with all races. I saw the whole problem as one big misunderstanding that could have been resolved through dialogue and friendship. I guess I felt that way because I had never had any trouble at all with white people. For me, segregation was more like a nagging headache than it was a stabbing pain.

When integration occurred, the superintendent, who was white, asked me if I had ever been around white children. I said, "I grew up with them in Yazoo County. The Cummings children were my best friends. I've been around them all my life." So that's the way it was. They picked me to teach at the Kirkpatrick School, and the first year of integration ended up being my last year of teaching.

It was a good experience. My whole family—my husband, myself, and my three kids—all got along with white people. One night my husband was driving

Lazy Summer Days
Clarksdale

up the highway going to work, and a white man stopped him and asked him for help. He said he was having trouble with his car, and he asked Charles to follow along behind him in case he broke down. Later, when Charles told him his name, he asked, "Are you related to Laura Hearn, the schoolteacher?"

Charles said, "Yes, she's my wife."

The man answered, "My kids had her in school, and they were just crazy about her."

Whenever I've had any kind of problem, I've turned to the church. I've always found solace and the solution to my problems in religion. I was raised in the First Baptist Church on Fourth Street. I started going to church there in 1925, and I've gone there ever since then. Reverend Self is our pastor. He lives in Memphis and drives down here. He was born and reared up in this church, just like I was, and he preaches a good sermon. We elected him to be our preacher. That's how it works in the Baptist church. Everyone has a vote, and you just vote on somebody, up or down. I taught Sunday school in that church for years, and now I'm the assistant superintendent. Mr. John Prentiss is our superintendent. He goes to the conventions and all the out-of-town events, and while he's gone I do his job. I volunteered, and the church accepted me.

We occasionally have a white visitor, but we don't have any white members. The other Baptist church, where Mr. Green preaches, has a few white members, but we don't. That doesn't bother me; I accept it. I've always believed in God, and when problems get so big on my mind that I can't throw them off, God says, "Save them all for Me."

Reverend Kent Bowlds

Former Pastor (1998–2003)
St. Elizabeth Catholic Church
Immaculate Conception Catholic Church • Clarksdale

I was born in 1956. I have a mother, father, four sisters, and one brother. I was raised Catholic. I went to Catholic grade school and high school. After high school, I went to Mississippi State and the University of Southern Mississippi and majored in communications. I worked for about ten years at a public broadcasting television station in Mississippi, but all during that time I thought about exploring the possibility of becoming a priest. Everybody who goes to seminary comes from different places with different attitudes. I was in my early thirties when I attended seminary at Theological College, part of Catholic University, in Washington, D.C., and in 1993, I was ordained as a priest.

My first parish was in Jackson, Mississippi, where I stayed for about four years. Then I went to Meridian, Mississippi, and I was there for about six months. Both of those assignments were as an associate pastor. Usually when you come out of seminary you go someplace to be an associate pastor, and you learn under other pastors. It is a well-established mentoring program. You can watch and observe and be mentored, but until you do it, you really don't have a real clear understanding of what it's all about. A good analogy is being married. You can study about it, you can read about it, and you can go to marriage-preparation classes, but until you're actually living it, you don't understand what marriage is all about. It's that way after you become an ordained deacon, and you start doing more. You start preaching and doing baptisms until you get a little bit clearer idea and then, as an associate pastor, you get even more of an idea. But all these are big leaps from seminarian to deacon, from deacon to priest, and from associate pastor to pastor.

Even now, I still make mistakes because I'm still learning. I try things that I think will work and they don't. I once had a dream where I was about to jump out of an airplane, then a voice said, "Don't worry; you're not doing it alone." A perfect example of this was our Bible study this morning. If I had gotten up in the pulpit and said, "We're going to start a Bible study. Someone will be here to teach you. Please come." It just would not have worked if it had been done that way, but it wasn't done that way. First, there was a whole team of people, who had been asking for it, and then they developed a team of leaders for the different Bible study groups. They took care of everything, like what to do with the children, what to do with babysitting, and what to do with hospitality, like coffee and donuts. Some of them even got up in the pulpit and talked about it. I

*"Even if people only come once a month, the thing
they come for is the celebration of the mass.
For us, we call it the source and the summit."*

promoted it, but it was a big success because I didn't try to do it alone—it was a team effort.

I guess what I like the least about the ministry is the administrative aspect. There are some days when I feel like I can't get away from my desk, because I'm dealing with things like the roof needing repair or planning some event that we're going to have. All of those things are necessary, but sometimes I feel like I didn't have to go to seminary for five years to learn how to do them. We have a bookkeeper and a receptionist here who help a lot, but I have to sign off on everything. Part of that is the way we're set up in the Catholic church. It's probably the same in a lot of denominations. The final say on a lot of things falls to the priest. That doesn't mean some administrative things aren't important; I just don't enjoy doing them.

What I like the most about my ministry is just being able to be with people. I was with a lady the other day that I hadn't seen for a long time, and she was quite ill. We do have people visiting hospitals and nursing homes and shut-ins at home because I can't do it all myself. It would be physically impossible because I have so many parishioners. Like just now, I was giving the sacrament of anointing to somebody who's going to have surgery this week, so this is a chance to anoint her and pray with her and her husband and their two kids. That's when I feel like I'm doing what I was called to do. For me, this is what the priesthood is all about.

Along with the joy of working with people also come the problems. I don't like having to deal with some of the tension that comes up. Like at Christmas, a time you'd think would be filled with lots of joy, happiness, and peace, but instead of that, people get all undone over the smallest details, like the flowers, or where to put the Christmas tree.

There's a lot of responsibility involved with this job. I've made some tremendous blunders. Sometimes I come down too hard on somebody, when I should have used a gentler or kinder approach. Maybe some of that's necessary, in order for me to learn, but I hate when things like that happen at the expense of someone else. What I do as a priest is all about people's souls; so if you do something well, somebody really appreciates it because you've touched them at the level of their soul. On the other hand, if you do something badly, you know you've hurt them at the level of their soul. That puts a lot of pressure on everything I do, and I have a lot to do!

In addition to running a K–8 school with 140 students, we also have an outreach ministry. We have a certain time when people come and receive assistance. We are able to help out a little bit with rent and utilities and things like that. People come, and we just sit down and talk about their problems. We have a group of people who interview people and talk with them one-on-one and see what their need is and help out a little bit with the light bill, or phone bill, or rent, or something like that. Immaculate Conception Church is a lot smaller, but there's a lot going on there. The membership is real small, so they can't be involved in a lot of things, but we rent what used to be the school over there to the Boys Club and Girls Club. That's a real necessary part of our ministry, because there are so many ways for kids to get into trouble with drugs, violence, and alcohol, that it gives them a place to go after school to do something positive.

September 11 was a day that presented a particular kind of problem. It was the day that we had scheduled our annual parish fair, and we talked all day about whether we should cancel it or not. In the end, we went ahead and had it because so much of it is geared toward kids, and it's not just something that's just for the parish. It's kind of an annual community event, and it's been going on for fifty years or more, and it really turned out to be a nice thing because people came together and we all stopped at the very beginning and held hands and said a prayer and sang the national anthem. You could just tell everybody had been glued to their television sets all day long, and this finally gave them a chance to get out and talk to one another and do something normal. We were determined not to let terrorism stop us from doing the things that we had always done. In a sense, it was almost an act of defiance on the parishioners' part. We tried to be respectful of what was going on, but at the same time we knew that our kids needed this, and we needed to show them that were not going to give in to the threat of terrorism. This was kind of a high point for my ministry.

One of the biggest low points has been the sexual scandals plaguing the church. I feel as though, at an institutional level, the church is working on the problem. We just got our new guidelines, and there'll probably be 70 to 100 pages of things that I can and can't do, should and shouldn't do, as far as employees or volunteers go. We are going to have to screen everyone now, and when there is a problem take it to the authorities and not just stop at the church level. Part of the problem is the time lag. A lot of these cases happened over twenty years ago, and the people who did things have not had the opportunity to go through the new programs the church has instituted. When I was in seminary, we talked a lot about celibacy, the implications of celibacy, and dealing with our own sexuality. These things weren't talked about in the seminary in years past when some of the guys were coming through who caused most of the problems.

We can't blame it all on the media and say they are picking on the church. The church is a human institution, and the people involved with the church make mistakes. I just have faith that, over time, God is going to correct what needs correcting, and God is going to suppress what needs suppressing, and He is going to raise up what needs raising up. In the end, it's going to be better, but it might be a rough road before we get there. In the meantime, we have the glory of the mass to see us through.

Sometimes when I'm leading mass, it hits me what the words really mean, and the people seem like they're really present to it and singing and praying, and even though it happens a lot, sometimes I pick up on it more than at other times. That's when I understand that we are all there for the same purpose—we're all there to receive something from God and give praise to God; when I feel that kind of unity of purpose, that's a really special time for me. I feel like the mass pulls all the disparate elements together, cinching them up, and allowing all of us to reach a religious pinnacle. Even if people only come once a month, the thing that they come for is the celebration of the mass. For us, we call it the source and the summit. It's the source of anything good that comes from receiving Jesus at the mass. And it's the summit, the place we come back to, where we give thanks to Jesus for whatever we have received.

Stained Glass Window
Episcopal Church
Vicksburg

Jack Perkins

Vice President, Sales and Marketing • Country Select Catfish Company
Isola

Back in 1975, we thought the industry was huge. There were only three or four plants at that time. Today, there are fifteen-plus plants processing catfish. But in that year, I think the entire industry processed a little less than 20,000,000 pounds of live catfish. This year, we'll do over 600,000,000 pounds of catfish. So the industry has grown tremendously. I remember the first time we processed 25,000 pounds of live catfish in one day; that was a number that we thought was astronomical. It was such a huge amount of fish, and we thought it would be years before we processed that many. But we did 25,000 in one day. At the end of the day, we cleaned the plant up, and the plant manager and myself and a couple of supervisors went and got a couple cases of beer. We sat out in the middle of the plant and drank the beer as our reward. Today, our plants are the largest in the industry, and we process 500,000 pounds of live fish every day. That shows how far the industry has come. At that time, we only had a total of 25 or 30 employees. But today, at this plant alone, we employ almost 1,200 people. We are a union plant, and we have really good relations with our union. Sometimes during the busy season, we may work six days in a week, but as a general rule we try to stick to the four-day week at one plant and five days at the other plant. Things have come a long way.

The local catfish farmers are the backbone of the industry. At one time, there were some large corporations involved in ownership or processing, but now almost all the plants are locally owned. Most of them are owned by stockholders who are fish farmers. There are some businessmen who own stock in some of the plants, but, for the most part, most of the processing plants are owned by catfish farmers. It's a situation that's very similar to the Farmers Co-Op. Most people are familiar with the way that works. The farmers are entrepreneurs who come up with their own capital to buy their land, their fish, their feed, and when they get fish ready to go to market, we buy their fish. That's what we do—we provide the trucks and process the fish. This industry and the way it's set up has made a lot of people wealthy, and it's broke a lot of people down to their knees. Overall, however, it's been a good industry for the Mississippi Delta, and we'd like to see it grow right here. This is the heart of it, and there is a lot of untapped growth capacity, both in production and sales. Imports are becoming a problem, especially in frozen markets. We'll deal with it. We'll continue to focus on growing our fresh retail sales and developing niche markets. The restaurant chains also offer a lot of potential for future growth.

"All I have to say is eat more catfish!"

We're pretty much at the mercy of market prices, but the only natural predator the fish have are birds, the cormorants. They're here from October through April, then they migrate, have little ones, and come back. They eat anywhere from one to three pounds of fish a day per bird. They're a real nuisance. On our farms we have to keep people in ATV's and pickup trucks running around the ponds during the winter, scaring the birds away. We keep them moving, because as soon as they land, they go under and come up with a fish. I've seen them swallow a ten- or twelve-inch fish! They swallow them head first, and then they fly off. If each bird only eats two or three fish a day, pretty soon it's eating into your profits. I can get a permit to kill some of them, but you can't kill very many. And there are so many birds that killing them isn't really practical. For now, the pickup trucks and ATV's seem to work the best. We also use gas-operated noise cannons, but the birds get used to them pretty quick. Most of the fish survive the birds, and when they do we process them.

The first step in the process is flavor testing. We do that a week or two before we harvest a pond. A farmer will bring fish in and we flavor test it; just like there are tasters in the wine industry and coffee industry, looking for the best grapes and the best coffee beans, we're looking for the best-tasting catfish. In order to make that happen, we make sure the fish are healthy fish and they taste good. Next, we'll harvest the fish. We go out to the farm with our trucks, which have water and aerators on them, and we load the fish onto the trucks alive. We keep the fish alive until they get back to the plant; it's just like processing hogs or cattle, we bring a live animal right to the door of the plant. It's very different from harvesting an ocean species, where fish may be caught out in the ocean, and it takes several days before it's brought back to be fully processed and packaged. As everybody knows, fresh fried chicken is the best thing you can get. The same is true with catfish—the fresher the better.

We bring the fish in and offload them from the live trucks. Occasionally, we may put them into a holding vat and keep them alive for several hours until we're ready to process them. We may be processing a larger or smaller fish at that time, so we don't need to run them through the plant right at that moment. Normally, however, we'll run the fish as soon as they get to the plant; they'll go right off the truck, right into the back door of the plant. They're beautiful channel catfish. They're blue and gray, sometimes with a greenish tint, but they are always a beautiful fish. The fish will usually average between one and three pounds. The ideal size fish would be a pound and a half to two pounds. If a farmer had his way, he'd sell his fish when they get to a pound and three quarters, and he wouldn't let them get over two pounds, because you don't get as good of a feed conversion when they get beyond that point. We have markets that demand different size fish. Some markets like large fish and some like small fish. But as a general rule, the live fish that we bring in average from one to three pounds.

Generally, we start with small fillets, in the two- to five-ounce range, which are primarily for restaurants and food-service wholesalers. Then we get into fillets that go up to ten, twelve, or even fifteen ounces. The larger fillets primarily go to retail supermarkets and seafood shops, where they like the larger fillets. In today's first run, we had about 250 people working at the initial processing site, which we call the slaughter room. This is where the processing begins, then the fish go from that stage immediately into an ice-water chill tank, because we want to be sure we get the fish chilled down as quickly as possible. All of this happens within just three to five minutes from when they come off the truck. They stay in the chill tank, in water that's almost freezing, for about thirty minutes. When the fillets come out, they're below 35 degrees. From that room, they go into the packaging room, where we start sizing them and separating what's going to retail and what's going to food service. The retail products usually go into a wax-coated, corrugated box, which we top with ice, much like the poultry industry. We make our own ice and we use tons of it every day.

Part of the reason we use so much ice is because of the distance to our markets. In our industry, we always refer to an area we call the heartland, a pear-shaped area, that stretches from Chicago, north of the Mississippi River, all the way down **Union**
Catfish Workers

to Oklahoma, Texas, and as far east as the Georgia coastal boundaries. Probably 75 percent of our catfish are sold in that bell-shaped region. But we are still shipping truckloads of catfish to New York, Boston, Miami, and California. We're sending catfish to every state in the Union; it may not be in your little neighborhood store, but that store could get it if they wanted to because there is a whole saler or distributor somewhere in its state that could bring catfish on a daily or weekly basis. The logistics of shipping fish to larger markets, say China, or Asia, or Europe, are more than we care to deal with right now. Just remember, if you live anywhere in the United States, farm-raised catfish is available, and we raise it right here in the Mississippi Delta. All I have to say is, "Eat more catfish!"

Jerry Lee "Duff" Dorrough

Musician and Artist • Ruleville

I can remember when I was four years old, sitting in Pete and Tootsie's Café, listening to Elvis Presley play "Hound Dog" on a record over and over again, then turning it over and playing "Don't Be Cruel." To this day, when I hear "Hound Dog," I can almost smell french fries, from spending all those hours in that restaurant listening to those songs. Even though I didn't like country music that much, my granddaddy was a big country music fan. He'd listen to the Grand Ole Opry every week, and whenever he could he'd take me to tent shows at Memphis and Ruleville. In the mid-1950s I saw the Everly Brothers, Patsy Cline, and some of the old-time country greats, but I was never a real fan of country music until I got older. But my mama remembered going to those country music package shows when Elvis, Scotty, and Bill were at the bottom of the bill. He was just part of an unknown front band then, playing to warm up the crowd for the stars. I always loved Little Richard, and I always loved Chuck Barry. I just loved rock 'n' roll! That's the bottom line for me.

I started listening to the Beatles when I was eleven, and my granddaddy, who always seemed to fit into the picture when you talk about music, took us to see the Beatles in 1966. That was right after John Lennon had made his comment about the Beatles being bigger than Jesus. Then they started having Beatle record burnings everywhere, but I wasn't about to burn any of my Beatles records. When we went to my cousin's house in East Memphis they said, "We're going to the youth rally for Christ tonight!" I'll never forget my granddaddy saying, "Well, we're going to see the Beatles." We went to the coliseum, but the Beatles didn't sell out the Mid-South Coliseum because of the uproar over John Lennon's remark, and the churches held a protest at the same time the concert was going on. I did love the Beatles, but I liked other music as well.

I can remember when I was in college at Delta State and Son Thomas came down, and some younger guys got him to play at a girls' dormitory. They knew I was a guitar player, so they asked me to come over and play with Son. We had a drink or two, and we hit it right off. Man, his guitar was tuned to something I had never heard, like something from outer space. I couldn't get with him. I couldn't get in tune. He'd be playing out of an open key or something, and I'd try to find it, but I never could. It really didn't make any difference to him. He could go from wherever he was to wherever he wanted to be. And he sang, too. He was really soulful, and then, after about three or four songs, he turned to me and said, "Now play me some of your blues."

"Now I realize that is what rock 'n' roll is—white boys trying to sing blues."

That's when I realized I'm a white kid, and I didn't have any blues! It took me a long time to realize that the music I loved came from right here—not down the road a little bit, but right here. It covered an area from New Orleans to Muscle Shoals, Alabama, over to Memphis and then back south again. One day a friend of mine gave me an instrumental record, *Talking the Blues,* by B. B. King, and that's when I started really getting into the blues.

After hearing B. B. King, and knowing he was from Indianola, I'd play his record over and over and try to work it up, and every once in a while I'd hit a few of those licks, so cool and jazzy and simple, and it would sound pretty good. But then I realized I needed to be a better singer, so I listened to more blues singers to learn their technique, and I tried to sing with more feeling.

One day, another college buddy took me to Club Ebony in Mound Bayou. The Club Ebony was on the chitlin' circuit, where black bands touring the area would stop and play. Even big name entertainers, like B. B. King, would stop for a night or two on their way through. That particular night we went to see the Bobby "Blue" Bland. I was a little apprehensive, because I knew it was going to be all African Americans, but this friend of mine, who was older, said it would be fine. Sure enough, after we got in there, some drunk tried messing with us, but two big black dudes came up and escorted him off. It was real cool.

Here it was 1970, and they let us stay there and dig Bobby "Blue" Bland, and Bobby Bland was great! I guess the first time I ever noticed the blues was in the 1960s. I fell in with some older guys, Tommy Free and his cousin Willie Free, and they were just two old white guys who lived in Ruleville. They sounded just great when they played, and they taught a lot of people around Ruleville to play the blues. All these little towns around here had a band; Drew had one; Cleveland was slap full of bands, and so was Greenwood. Every town that size had kids getting up bands, and that's the way I came up.

About that time the coaches wanted me to go out for football, but I was making forty dollars a night at the youth center, and I wasn't about to go out there and break my fingers. So I started on drums, graduated to bass, and finally started playing guitar. I was real fortunate, and later on, my old band, the Tangents, went out west, and people would ask us to play Delta blues. Charlie "Love" Jacobs told them, "We play bluesy music, but Delta Blues is an older kind of acoustic music, and we don't do that." Then we'd turn around and play a Ray Charles or Duke Ellington song. I think me and Charlie, for white boys, were pretty passable singers. We certainly weren't blues singers, but we tried to sing with feeling. Now I realize that is what rock 'n' roll really is—white boys trying to sing the blues. A lot of our heroes were the great black singers, like Otis Redding, Wilson Pickett, and James Brown, and pretty soon it gets to where it's like a gumbo; whatever you put in there, the flavor starts to come out. What we played was called soul music or rhythm and blues, but it wasn't the old-time, field hand blues. Jerry Wexler, sometimes credited with coining the phrase rhythm and blues, said years later he wished he'd called it rhythm and gospel. He said that because soul music seemed to come out of the church, and that all the great soul singers were also great gospel singers.

I noticed early on that black churches were a lot different than my church. When I go to my little Methodist church up here, folks there really hate to show any emotion, and they hate to speak out. In a black church, it's just the opposite. We've had black pastors come in and preach, and our area coordinator is a black pastor.

When he's here you might get a few amen's here and there, but when you go to a black church, it lasts all day, and they just let everything out and it's wonderful. I think their service developed that way because the black church was the only place where they had real privacy, and where they could practice their sacred rituals. But I have to respect both of them, black and white, because they are both sacred.

Funerals are also big in the black community. Sarah, an old gal I'd known all my life, died recently. She had a house close to here where she took care of the old black men. They'd come by and she'd cook for them, and she sold a little bootleg gin on the side, and when I got old enough to drink, I would go to Sarah's place with my friends, and we would party with her. When she died, they buried Sarah at the Mount Layton Baptist Church. I went down there. I knew a lot of the folks, and the preacher was from Shelby. He was good man and a fiery speaker. He gave her a real send off, kind of like a combination wake, revival, and song service. With all the singing and praying, it was more like a celebration than a funeral. It was like a New Orleans funeral. They didn't have a parade, but the service went all day, and it was just real heartfelt, with a lot of feeling. When the preacher preached and sang you could hear the bluesy cadence in his voice.

After the service, I told him I could hear them singing when they held their weekly services; their voices would float across the fields. He invited me to come and worship with them, and at first I agreed, but then I decided it might make someone uncomfortable, and if I made just one person feel uncomfortable, then I didn't want to go to the service. I did, however, appreciate the singing, and the history of the old-time blues and gospel music.

Strangely enough, I didn't see many younger black kids getting into playing or singing the blues. It was almost as if they perceived it as a shameful thing, or something that turned them off because it brought back bad memories, or not necessarily bad memories, but it had a bad connotation. For instance, they didn't want to listen to those old records and work up some Big Bill Broonzy or any of the other old-timers. Then I realized that the harsh things that created blues as a music form, to a large degree, no longer existed: slavery, field bosses, sharecroppers, chain gangs, and chopping cotton were all gone.

I've got a friend, Vasti Jackson, who kind of illustrates what was happening with the younger players. He was the kind of rock player who could really play Steely Dan. But he got affiliated with Z. Z. Hill, a gospel singer turned blues singer, which is the best kind of singer because gospel is truly roots music. Z. Z.

Hill was a fantastic singer, and he had big success with "Down Home Blues," and he's the one who put Malaco Records on the map. Malaco Records is the largest independent record company in the world, right here in Jackson, Mississippi. They've got Bobby "Blue" Bland, Little Milton, Z. Z. Hill before he died, Denise LaSalle, and a whole lot more heavy-duty artists, like my friend Vasti. He went from being more of a rock player to getting into the blues in his late twenties and thirties. He was a real talent, and it was weird watching that happen. There was a kind of slacking-off period from the old-time blues, and then there was a resurgence of the old music. I guess Vast is living proof of that trend.

My artwork sort of happened the same way my music did. I was just one of those kids who loved to draw. Kids are the best artists. I always loved a pencil, even loved the way they smelled. I bet I'd eat them sons of bitches if I could. There weren't any art classes in Ruleville Public School, so I would go to the library and check out every art book in the library. We'd seen all those art books and we checked all of them out two or three times. Kids really aren't ready to study art until they're just about out of high school. All through high school they think they know all there is to know, and you can't teach them anything. That's pretty much the attitude I had, so I wasn't very teachable. I would find out what my buddies were drawing, and if they were drawing cowboys, then I drew cowboys. And we could all draw cartoon characters, and I had friends who drew big war scenes, but I wasn't into that kind of art. When I finally got to college, I was sitting in drawing class, and the old boy teaching the class, Sammy Britt, was from Ruleville!

He said, "Yeah, I bet some of ya'll were probably the best artists in your whole school, weren't ya? I bet ya'll really thought you was something."

Boy, he cut us off at the knees. Then he said, "This semester you're all going to learn what you don't know."

He proceeded to teach us about light and shadow, shading and depth, and then he translated that to color and he showed us slides of other people's work, and it was like looking at diamonds for the first time. Sammy was a real color freak, but he came by it natural.

His teacher was Henry Hensche, who had studied with Charles Hawthorne, who had studied under William Merritt Chase, who had actually painted with Claude Monet. From Sammy Britt back to Claude Monet there was a direct link to the impressionists. What Sammy taught and what he learned from Mr. Hensche was a combination of the bold color of the impressionists, combined with the solid drawing technique of the Old Masters. I discovered that not drawing something and filling it in, but giving it shape and form with spots of color was really a simple but profound way of looking at things. From there, he said, "Now, all of you just go and do what you want to do." He didn't want us to paint like him, or to imitate his work the way a lot of students do with their teachers. He just wanted us to paint the way we see the world.

Pat Ryan

Flying Y Aero • Tutwiler

I've been crop dusting for nearly thirty-five years, but I don't know how much longer it will last. We constantly have to deal with environmental regulations, and they are a big threat to the industry, but an even bigger threat is genetically engineered seed. They've already developed a cotton plant that has some tolerance to the boll worm. They could develop a seed that doesn't need fertilizer or weed control. When that happens, we'll be in the same shape that the industry is in England and Sweden. In England, there are only two operators left. It's not against the law to spray there, but there are so many laws about how you are supposed to do it, people just threw up their hands and quit. It simply wasn't worth the aggravation. It's the same way in Sweden. Sweden has huge forests, and they used to do a lot of crop dusting there. Now, about all they'll let them put down is fertilizer. They won't let them spray any insecticides at all. Between the regulators and the new seeds coming out, the industry could be in real trouble ten or fifteen years down the road. It won't affect me, because I'll be retired by then, but it will affect the next generation of crop dusters.

I fly an Ayres Turbo Thrush. They are built in Albany, Georgia, and a brand new one would cost about $500,000. This plane has a three-bladed propeller, which allows it to maintain constant speed, and the power plant is a Dash 27 Pratt and Whitney gas turbine engine that produces 750 horsepower. We work these airplanes awfully hard, and we know we have to take care of them because our lives depend on it. To make sure they are working properly, the engine has to be checked and recertified after every 1,200 hours of flying. First they open up the engine and do what is called a hot section, which means they check all of the components in the "hot" part of the engine—the pistons, valves, etc.—where the power is generated.

They also check the blade length, and they look for any parts that are worn out and need replacing. At my last major inspection, they replaced a vein ring, and that cost about $9,000. They also told me I was going to have to put new blades on the turbine wheel the next time, and that was going to cost about $15,000. It costs $4,500 just to open up the motor and check it out, whether they find anything wrong or not. If there's nothing wrong, they put on new gaskets, clean the nozzles, do a proficiency check on the engine, and after they put it back together, the airplane is ready to operate for another 1,200 hours. These planes are built to perform under extreme conditions.

"We get paid by the acre, and, with those kind of expenses,
if we're not flying we're not making any money."

The Thrush can haul 400 gallons of liquid, or 3,000 pounds of fertilizer, per run. The two fuel tanks are in the wings, 115 gallons in each wing, and the plane is equipped with a GPS locator. We know where we are, but the locator allows us to go back to the exact spot where we stopped spraying in the field at the end of one run and lay down another swathe without any overlap. The loading crew has a load sheet that shows exactly how many runs you need to make, and how many gallons of spray you need to carry on each run. When you're finished, they run pure water to clean out the entire system before you change over to something else. We rarely load the plane completely full, because when we do it doesn't fly very well.

When we get in the air, we fly at about 145 mph, and spray about twelve feet off the ground, using rotary micronaire atomizers. That's when we get our best dispersal, but a whole lot has to happen before we even get in the air. Each one of these planes carries $35,000 in insurance (and $10,000 in liability insurance) just in case we spray the wrong field and it damages or kills someone's crop. After you add in the maintenance and insurance for the aircraft, that's about 25 percent of the gross. The season lasts from mid-March to early October, and I'm usually

Art Imitates Life, mural by Cristen Craven Barnard

in the air at daylight trying to beat the wind. We get paid by the acre, and, with those kind of expenses, if we're not flying we're not making any money.

People need to understand that crop dusting isn't as dangerous as it used to be. It is probably the country's most regulated industry. We have to maintain a closed system, which means that all of the poison is kept inside the containers it arrives in. When we're ready to us it, we use a special apparatus that sucks the chemicals out of the containers and into the mixing vat. The mixing vat lid can be opened, but it is usually closed so that none of the poison will escape into the air while it is being mixed. My loader wears a respirator, goggles, an apron, and gloves, which protect him from any exposure to the chemicals. When he pumps the chemicals into the aircraft, the liquid flows through plastic, see-through tubing, which keeps it away from the pilot.

Even if a few drops escape and fall on the ground, they land on a concrete pad that can be washed off, and the residue is then put into a special holding tank. We try to make sure that none of the contaminants go anywhere except where they are supposed to go—on the fields. That is what's called a closed system, and it actually works pretty well. The most important part of the whole operation, however, is the airplane itself. These aircraft are very special. I hope we don't go the way of Sweden and England and virtually eliminate crop dusting, because airplanes and helicopters, in many instances, are the only things that farmers have to get the job done.

Brenda Denise Wilson

Blackjack Dealer • Grand Casino • Tunica

I've been a blackjack dealer here for two years. I was a part-time dealer at the Sheraton, but after the Grand opened, I came here. The training only takes about four weeks. I spent three weeks learning how to deal the game, the procedures and so forth, then the fourth week, I worked with the customers. I've been working this shift since I started at the Grand, a little over two years ago. The swing shift is really good for me because it allows me to go to school. I recently finished my Bachelor of Arts in English literature at Jackson State University. Right now I'm pursuing a Master of Arts in English literature at the University of Memphis. I eventually want to be a college professor, but for now, this pays more than a minimum-wage job. You'd probably be surprised to find out that most people who work in the casinos are not even from Tunica. Many of the workers are from Memphis or Helena, Arkansas. Some people from Tunica take advantage of the entertainment offered at the casinos, but it's not a real big thing as far as jobs go, because they have other things they like to do. A lot of people from Tunica either go off to college, or they just leave home to do other things.

At first, a lot of people, including me, had negative ideas about the casinos. I guess it was because the casinos were something new and different. The first thing we thought about casinos was that they were here to take money. That's what a lot of us thought. They're just going to come here, take all the money they can from Tunica, then leave. We didn't think they would do anything good for Tunica County. But after watching them for several years, it became apparent they were doing a lot for Tunica. Not only were they giving people jobs, new schools started to go up, and they provided the financial resources so that people could get better housing. And it's not just Tunica. They're doing a lot of stuff in Memphis. They changed a lot of people's minds, including mine. They are doing much better than I thought they ever would, and the environment inside and outside the casinos is quite nice, and I meet all kinds of people.

I meet doctors, lawyers, rich people, middle class, poor people, friendly people, and angry people. I strike up a conversation, and I'm often surprised at the things we have in common. I meet a lot of college students who are working on their degrees, and I've also had lots of compulsive gamblers and card counters come to my table. I can always spot the compulsive gamblers.

One sign is they want to win every hand, and they are constantly complaining. Real gamblers know that they are taking a chance whenever they put their money on the table. Real gambler know that they have to take the good with

*"Card counters usually start betting a $5 hand,
and the cards are lousy for them. Then all of the sudden
they bet $5,000 and they start winning."*

Roulette

the bad, that the cards are not going to always fall right, but they're not always going to be bad, either. Deep down inside, compulsive gamblers want to lose. That's why they constantly complain, even when they're winning, because that matches their low self-esteem. Counters are something totally different. Card counters usually start betting a $5 hand, and the cards are lousy for them. Then all of the sudden they bet $5,000, and they start winning. What they're trying to do is change the odds so they're drastically in their favor.

When that happens I can tell they're counting the cards. To be honest, I'm not sure whether it's legal or illegal, but I had a card counter at my table, and I told my supervisor, but my supervisor told me he couldn't really do anything about it. I did what I could; I started shuffling every hand, and I asked another dealer to trade out with me. I tried to break his concentration, because you have to really stay focused, for a very long period of time, when you're counting cards.

I rarely have anyone try to cheat, but occasionally, when one of my compulsive gamblers keeps losing bigger and bigger, I tell them they need help, but they don't listen and they get verbally abusive. Then, instead of trying to beat the cards, they personalize it and try to beat me, and they get mad and call me names. I don't personalize it because I don't have any money on the table. As long as they don't physically touch me it's OK, but if they touch me, I call security. The positive aspects of my job far outweigh the negative ones. I like my job a lot!

George Walker

Former President • Delta Wire Company • Clarksdale

The steel wire business traditionally came to the United States from Europe, primarily Sweden and Germany. When it arrived in America it was centered in Massachusetts. I was president of a wire company there that had plants in Los Angeles, California, Akron, Ohio, and Worcester, Massachusetts. About twenty years ago, in the early 1980s, we felt the need for a southern plant due to markets that were switching to the South. I asked Harvard Business School to find a location for a southern plant, and after compiling a four-hundred-page report filled with facts and figures, they drew a map. It basically stretched from Olive Branch, to Greenwood, over to Greenville, from there to Rosedale, then to Cleveland, Clarksdale, and back up to the Tennessee line. I came down with that study in my briefcase, and we went around with the various economic development people. When we came to Clarksdale we were impressed because they had a building, and we wanted to get started. When we saw the favorable freight alliances we could make, we moved down here from Massachusetts and started a small company. The rest of the story is that after we got started, the world got a whole lot more complicated, more competitive, and there were greater demands on products and people to produce them. I went to Jackson, our state capital, and arranged some training for our people.

The state administrators responded admirably; they set up training for their community college teachers, even sending some of them to Ohio and Massachusetts, so they could come back to Coahoma Community College, here in Clarksdale, and Mississippi Delta Community College in Moorhead, which is about fifty miles from here, and set up courses to train our employees. These weren't easy courses. They were similar to college statistics courses, and we had to teach them to an indigenous population that had never accepted such a challenge. Not everybody could or would accept this idea, so our first job was to convince them they could do it. The vast majority of them accepted the challenge, and they worked hard.

As a result, we have become somewhat of a model, even though we are the smallest company in the wire-making business; we have less than 200 employees, and three of our chief competitors, all foreign-owned, have many more employees. One in Belgium employs 25,000 people; one in England employs over 12,000; and there's also a Canadian company that employs 7,000. One of our customers, Goodyear Tire and Rubber Company, gives a Best of Class worldwide award. Two out of the past three years that award has gone to Delta Wire. We won the award

"We made that wire by taking an unemployed agricultural group of people and turning them into a highly skilled, well-trained, well-paid, industrial workforce."

because of our company philosophy. We don't believe in layoffs, and we produce a very, very high-quality product, right here in Clarksdale, Mississippi. We've achieved such a high degree of success for several reasons.

The first reason was that we developed a participative management style that is created in plant meetings. That type of thing is in vogue right now, but we were doing it before anyone even heard about the concept, simply because it seemed to be the smart thing to do. No one ever heard of doing it in Boston, much less Clarksdale, Mississippi. The second reason is because we promote from within the company. Our plant manager at Delta Wire is an African American, our maintenance manager is an African American, and three out of five supervisors are African Americans. In a way, we have been a beacon to some management practices that work excellently for Delta Wire and have, indeed, been emulated all over the United States and even in other parts of the world. We are a state-of-the-art facility, and we make a product that is not easy to make. Primarily, we make steel wire for automobile tires, airplane tires, and wire that is used in undersea cable for telephones and telegraphs.

We start out with a quarter-inch steel rod, and we bring it down to an average size of .037 inches, which has been reduced, over and over again, without using any heat. If you anneal something, which means you roll it red hot, it comes out very, very soft. The wire we make, because it is cold-worked, increases in tensile, which means our wire is very, very strong; it takes a tremendous force to break it or to twist it. Even though plastics and many other things have come out which have replaced or replicated many other products, nothing has ever replicated the steel wire for the purposes for which we use it. Imagine you are driving a tractor-trailer truck with a twenty-ton load, or a 747 airplane that's about to land. Something's going to have to provide the necessary strength to keep those tires on the wheel. We make the wire that is in those tires, and we made that wire by taking an unemployed agricultural group of people and turning them into a highly skilled, well-trained, well-paid, industrial work force.

The machines we use here are state-of-the-art. Since we are the smallest company, our equipment has to be the best. It's also very capital intensive: about the least expensive machine we would buy would cost about a million and a half dollars, or even more. All of our machines are computer controlled. They are all automatic, very sophisticated, and they are self-diagnostic. Many of them are robotic. These machines are no longer made in the United States, so if we wanted the manufacturer to maintain them, we would have to pay someone to make a service call from Germany, Italy, or France, just to fix them every time a machine broke down, and that's no way to make money. That's why we have trained our people not just to run all of our machines but to fix them as well. This has worked out very well for the company and for the employees as well. Our people are non-union, but they have a pretty good deal in terms of pay.

Our employees know they are going to get four days' pay a week, whether they work or not. Beyond that, they get what I call a productivity and quality incentive plan. This basically puts in each person's hands, on a cooperative basis, what they're going to make. On these large machines, we all know what degree of efficiency each one of them can reach. So the workers know that they will be directly compensated for their efforts. A lot of people think we came South for low labor rates, but we've never had low labor rates—and, in fact, we don't want them. The way we are set up, the workers average twelve or thirteen dollars an hour. Some make more, some make less, depending on how hard each employee is willing to work. The harder they work, the more money they make, and the more money they make, the more money Delta Wire makes. It is a win-win situation. We also provide our workers with full benefits; we were the first company in the state to offer our people not just medical but dental benefits as well. The whole system is based on self-motivation and motivation from other employees.

The self-motivating part of this quality and productivity plan is that everyone here can see a direct connection between productivity and payday. If things start piling up, no one calls the foreman. One of the workers whose saving for a new car or a new house may step in and say, "Hey, let me help you out here. We need to straighten this mess out and get the line moving. We need to make our incentive this week!"

The quality part of the plan works more or less the same way. If the line starts turning out product that doesn't pass quality-control checks, then it is subtracted from the weekly incentive pay. Everyone in this plant understands that there are direct connections between motivation, training, production, incentive, quality, and payday. Even though I am the boss, the captain of the ship so to speak, I rarely have to say anything to the workers. They take care of most of the problems themselves. The people in Clarksdale are proud of this plant and so am I. When I walk around town, half the people I see are wearing a Delta Wire cap, and we don't have that many employees. Any employee who wants a Delta Wire cap, or T-shirt, gets it for free. The people I see say, "My husband works at Delta Wire, or my Mom or my Dad works there," and you can see that they are very proud of that fact. As a result of the success we have had at Delta Wire, I am helping replicate our business model all over the state of Mississippi. In fact, five states—Florida, South Carolina, Arkansas, Alabama, and Louisiana, have copied our Work Force Training Act of 1994 and are emulating what we have done here in their states.

As I said, even though I am semi-retired, I am just about a full-time, unpaid volunteer for the state of Mississippi. I am chairman of the Community College Board, and we operate fifteen community colleges with 150,000 students. I'm also on the Department of Economic Development board and the Enterprise Corporation for the Delta, which provides working capital for loans, particularly for minority entrepreneurs. One of our minority applicants is working to create a laundry that will do all the laundry for all the hotels and casinos at Tunica. It will employ seventy-five people and will have a two-million-dollar payroll. There are two people overseeing the startup of this company, and one of them is me.

The Delta is a beautiful place, and we have destroyed a lot of stereotypes since we moved here over twenty years ago. The people here are good people, and, with the right opportunity and training, they can succeed at anything. I honestly feel anything you want to do can be done in the Delta, if you do it right. That's my belief, and I still have the ownership of my company to prove it. The other proof I have is that it's not necessary for me to be at the plant everyday because the people I have trained run the place. My wife and I are free to live anywhere in the world, but we have made the decision to stay here, even though we have a bigger house in Maine. We want to stay here because of the people and because of all the good things that are happening in the Delta.

Best Wire in the South
Delta Wire Company

Dr. Van R. Burnham

Physician • Clarksdale

I was born in Marks, Mississippi, in 1920, and my father was a dentist who practiced there. My mother and father had a two-story home they ordered from Sears and Roebuck, which was shipped in by train, on flatcar and boxcar. It was put together by a carpenter in Marks, and I think there were two or three other houses that were prefabricated and shipped into Marks during 1917 and 1918. The house is still standing and in beautiful shape. Then 1922 came, and cotton fell from a dollar a pound to five cents a pound. My father lost everything.

We moved to Ruleville in 1923, and our world was very segregated. The schools were segregated—white schools, black schools, and even a Chinese boarding school at Cleveland for the Asian students. It was the same way in health care. After my father started private practice again, he worked on both white and black patients, but everything was separate. His patients waited in a long reception area to be treated, and it was clearly marked where each group was supposed to sit. He also had different treatment rooms for each group; he had the white room, which was a little nicer than the room where he treated his black patients, and the equipment was more modern than what he had in the other room. The primary reason for the separation was the instruments. He had two completely different sets of instruments—one for white patients, and one for black patients. It was just a totally different world back then—one that was totally segregated, one that you didn't even think about and we just accepted it. It was part of life.

I grew up in Ruleville, but my Delta roots involve a lot of the social structure here in the Delta; I went to teen parties and dances all over the Mississippi Delta, where everyone knew everyone else. If someone was having a party of some sort next month, invitations would be sent out to young people all over the Delta. We would RSVP and show up on the appropriate day and at the appropriate time. They would have music by Kay Kaiser, or the State Band, or the Rebel Ramblers. It was a very friendly, really going thing. You got to know everybody all over the Delta. I wouldn't change a thing about how I grew up in these small towns in the Delta.

After I graduated from Ruleville High School, I went to Sunflower Junior College for two years. Dormitory life was a great experience, although there were restrictions like you would not believe. While I was at Sunflower I organized a junior varsity football team. Even though I was the smallest one on the team, I was the quarterback and captain. We just played some of the high school teams,

"I practiced medicine for 62 years; I retired on January 1, 2005."

like Greenwood and Greenville. But they gave me a ten-dollar-a-month scholarship for playing sports, and school cost seventeen dollars a month. That little scholarship enabled me to finish my first two years at college, and then I transferred to Ole Miss, where I received my undergraduate degree, and went to the two year medical school at Oxford.

While I was a sophomore in medical school at Ole Miss, one sunny Sunday morning, we were having a doctor-lawyer football practice. That was Pearl Harbor day. The next week the army and navy recruiters were in town, and a bunch of us went down to volunteer. Some of the boys went into the army, but a bunch of us went into the navy. They gave us our commissions in April, in the U.S. Naval Reserve, and told us we were right where we were supposed to be, and to keep going to college. We were second year medical students. Two years later, in 1942, I finished my medical training at Northwestern in Chicago, but while I was training I had a very strange experience.

During the war, and even before, because of mechanization, all the tenant farmers left the Delta and went North to Detroit and Chicago. I guess that's one of the reasons I went to Northwestern, because I was just following the trend. After a while I was assigned obstetrical duty at the maternity center. They gave us two weeks' training and taught us how to deliver babies in the home. Pretty soon I was riding a streetcar to the South Side of Chicago, carrying my medical bag and wearing my little white jacket, ready to deliver babies in the home. After I delivered my first baby, a healthy black boy, I was filling out the papers and asked the mother where she was born. She said, "I was born in Mississippi."

Then I said, "I was born in Mississippi, too." And I asked, "Whereabouts in Mississippi?"

And she said, "Ruleville."

I was flabbergasted. "By Gosh, I'm from Ruleville too. Where were you born?"

She answered, "On Mr. Bootsie Barner's place."

And I said, "Mr. Bootsie Barner is one of my daddy and mamma's best friends. He was at their house the other day." I thought it was very strange that the first baby I delivered in Chicago belonged to a woman from Ruleville, Mississippi, my hometown.

When I finished my studies in Chicago, I did my residency at Pennsylvania Hospital in Philadelphia. It is the oldest hospital in America, and it is very prestigious. When I left Philadelphia, I shipped out of San Francisco on a troop ship with 5,000 marines and 92 doctors. We were headed West toward Japan, and were to have been ready to attack the Japanese homeland. But three days after we went to sea, V-J Day happened, and we knew we were going to survive the war, but we didn't let down our guard. We zigzagged to keep any submarines from hitting us, and I stayed overseas for twelve months.

First I went to Manila, then to Shanghai, and finally I went to Kowloon, which is right next door to Hong Kong. The Nationalist Army had the Chinese communists backed up into the ocean and were going to annihilate them. We went down and rescued the communists; I think there were six landing ship tanks that took 30,000 more communists off the beach and took them up to Korea to reinforce the communist garrison there. They gave us a wing ding of a party up there in Tsingta. I was discharged from the navy in 1946, but later had eighteen months of service during the Korean War as a lieutenant commander, all served stateside.

After I was discharged from my WW II service in 1946, I spent two years of general practice in Vaiden, Mississippi, where the resident doctor had been killed in a automobile accident. Vaiden was a little hill town with gravel roads and muddy roads. While I was there, I made a lot of house calls. Once I made a house call in a rowboat, once or more on a mule, and I made many on the back end of a tractor. But I was usually able to use my car; I had a little '34 two-door Ford Roadster. It would scoot like mad, but it was always getting stuck in the mud or in a pothole. When it did, I'd just take the jack and put it under the wheel that was stuck, start the motor, go forward, and then go back and pick up the jack. Then I'd wipe the mud off of me and the car and keep on going down the road until I got stuck again. It was a pretty good way to travel, slipping and sliding on those clay roads out in the country. When I was young and feisty, I knocked down a lot of mail boxes, zooming around curves. I'm glad it was fun, because it sure didn't pay very much.

One night I spent ten or twelve hours delivering a little black baby, and all I got was a bucket of molasses. And of course I occasionally got chickens. Office calls were $2.00, and delivering a baby at home cost $25. After I moved to Clarksdale and started practice with an older doctor, Dr. Carr, the conditions weren't as crude, but the price was the same: $25 for a home delivery. And, of course, most of the babies I delivered in the home in Clarksdale were black. I delivered a few white babies in the home, but they had a white hospital here, and a lot of the white women went to the hospital. Still, even with the hospital, quite a few white women had their babies at home. I charged them the same: $25 for a home delivery, or $50 for a delivery in the hospital. In the Delta, payment for my services was always a peculiar subject.

When I first came to Clarksdale, the farmers and the plantation owners would all pay in the fall, after the harvest. I'd wait on their tenants throughout the year, and they'd pay me in September, October, or November. I just carried them on the books until then. When I'd present them with a $150 bill they would take 10 percent off because they were paying in cash, even though I had carried them all year. Then they'd charge their tenant $150 plus 10 percent, and the tenant couldn't do anything about the situation. But I could. It made me very angry, and after my first year in Clarksdale, I refused to accept anything less than full payment.

I had one farm owner who called me out, and I delivered a baby on his place and charged him $50, because I had to do an episiotomy by lamplight and then sew her back up again. He raised hell. He said he had never paid more than $25, and he wasn't going to pay it this time; I never did wait on his people again. I tried to explain the situation to him, but he absolutely refused to listen.

The biggest change I've seen in medicine is the availability of antibiotics. Prior to the discovery of antibiotics, mastoiditis, pneumonia, and other infections were all very hard to treat, and it was just terrible. Over the years I've learned that antibiotics keep down so many secondary infections before they become serious. I give my patients antibiotics to keep them from getting complications. The other thing that has changed is house calls. I now make only six or eight house calls a year. Patients usually come to the office now, but back when I first started, the doctor went to the patient daily and even on Sunday. Reducing house calls made a difference; I could see a lot more patients and provide better care.

I would like to comment on the changes that have occurred in medical practice since I received my medical degree in December 1943 and retired on January 1, 2005. There is no longer any segregation in the medical field, with complete integration in every facet. For my part, medical practice changed from an office-home type to an office-hospital relationship with patients. Scientific advances have not only introduced antibiotics but all kinds of treatment and diagnostic modalities that have increased the lifespan of the American people. I believe continuing research and its application give this country a bright future.

Yearly Checkup
Dr. Burnham's
Examination Room

Lana Draper Turnbull

Former Director • Communications and Community Relations
Northwest Mississippi Regional Medical Center • Clarksdale

I grew up in Merigold, Mississippi. In college, I majored in social work, and after I graduated, my new husband and I moved to Nashville, Tennessee. He was in the music business, so that seemed like the place to go. I stayed in Nashville for twenty-one years, and that's where I got involved with marketing and communications. I worked with architecture and engineering firms, commercial real estate firms, and landscape architects.

After working there for about twenty years, I started to come back to the Delta more often to visit. My son was reaching an age where I wanted him to get to know his cousins and all his relatives in Mississippi. And eventually I discovered that every time I came back for a visit it got harder and harder to leave. I used to go through what I called post-Delta depression. I missed having everybody around me that I knew, people who liked to hug me and be just really close and friendly. After several years of this, I decided to start looking for possible jobs back in the Delta and went on a letter-writing campaign. After about six months, I was able to pull together enough consulting work to allow me to make a living and move back to my hometown, Merigold. I really enjoy the small town setting, and there's just something special about the Delta; something that draws you back in once you leave. I also thought this was the time that things could actually start changing, and that the Delta could grow.

When I came home, I worked at the hospital for six months as a consultant. I primarily wrote articles for the newspaper. When I started as a full-time employee, my new job was to fill a typical marketing role. I tried to get some advertising started, and I tried to do some community outreach. But when the hospital was sold to Health Management Associates of Naples, Florida, things changed rapidly. HMA is a for-profit hospital chain that owns thirty-five hospitals in the Southeast. Along with a new owner came a new administration, and they wanted to expand my role.

They were very anxious to see construction that had been started on the hospital completed, and they wanted to change the whole image of the institution. As a county hospital, there had been limited funds in terms of marketing and in terms of the renovations for the amenities that could be added to the hospital. In the past, employees pretty much did their jobs within the walls of the hospital, and there was not a lot of coordinating with the larger community. The new administrator, David McCormick, changed that in a hurry.

"There was one gentleman we screened for the city of Clarksdale, and when the nurse took his blood pressure, she realized he was in the process of having a heart attack. If it hadn't been for us he would have died."

David was anxious to see the hospital become involved in the community, in various organizations and groups all over town. We became involved in everything from race relations to economic development, to improving education. Through David, I got involved in those groups, too, so I got in on the ground floor of all the changes. I became very involved with the chamber of commerce, and that's been something I really enjoy. It was important that the hospital be seen as a friend to the community, not just a place to go when you are sick. We became a resource, and we really stepped up our community outreach.

This new policy changed how people felt about the hospital. I'm proud to say that the hospital is now very much a positive influence in the community—one that looks toward the future rather than the past. I think the way of the future for the Mississippi Delta has got to be education. It has got to focus on disease and illness prevention, rather than on trying to cure disease when it is full blown. Health care institutions must be a part of that educational process.

The hospital sponsors, along with Delta Partners of Care, community health screens several times a year. We also have a occupational medicine program, where we go out to industries and businesses and do free health screening for their employees. That helps them reduce their insurance rates and it also helps identify some of their employees who are at very high risk for stroke, diabetes, or heart attacks.

There was one gentleman we screened for the city of Clarksdale, and when the nurse took his blood pressure, she realized he was in the process of having a heart attack. He probably wouldn't have lived through the day, but we were able to get an ambulance, take him to the emergency room, get him in the critical-care unit, and now he's on a program of diet, exercise, and medicine. He's doing just fine. Not every case is that dramatic, but it illustrates how very rewarding it is for the people who have been involved in disease prevention, when they see how they can really make a difference in someone's life.

We do the same thing for the children. We have a health fair for kids, and we have discovered that there are third-graders in this community with high blood pressure. We try to start early and educate them about ways to live healthier, happier lives based on diet and exercise. We see our role as community involvement and disease prevention as opposed to disease cure. There is a much better return for dollars spent in prevention than there is for dollars spent on treatment. It's kind of like the old car commercial: we can change your oil now, or rebuild your motor later. That is more or less the choice we've made, and here at the hospital we are in the oil-changing business. I am also involved in lots of organizational work outside the hospital, on my own time.

When I moved back to the Delta, I knew I'd always liked the blues, but I didn't know very much about the music. After I moved back here I decided to take my son to the Delta Blues Museum and let him learn a little bit more about the music that started here and put this place on the map. The more I learned about the blues the more I liked it, and although I had been to one festival, I had not been involved in any of the organizational aspects until last year. I was invited to come to one of the meetings for the Blues Festival, and before I knew it (I don't really remember volunteering), I somehow left the meeting as a committee chair.

I got involved as the chair for backstage hospitality, and that's really been a lot of fun. It's a very diverse group. I've got to meet a lot of people I wouldn't have met otherwise, and I've gotten to meet the artists. I also get to help play a part in being sure that the festival doesn't lose its Delta flavor. That's so important. We have the real thing here, and I don't want us to lose that, but a lot of the older bluesmen are passing away, and I feel really fortunate that during the past couple of years I've gotten to know some of the old blues players.

Winding Staircase
Duff Mansion
Vicksburg

Even though I don't live in Coahoma County, I can see it is on the verge of having so many exciting things happen. I think sometimes our own community forgets there are people who save for their vacation all year to come from Australia, Norway, and New Zealand, and this is a very important place to them in terms of their love of music. We have a great opportunity to show them our heritage. We're also about to be in a transportation corridor that's going to open up more opportunities for business and industry to come into the area. People are working together in a way they've never worked together before; different churches, races, and socioeconomic groups are all coming together because we now realize much more unites us than divides us. It excites me because we've been through some downturns during the last few years, but I really think all that is changing; in the future, Clarksdale is going to be an up-and-coming place, an exciting place, a place where we can show the world that the old Delta magic still exists!

Olenza Self McBride

Principal • Clarksdale High School • Clarksdale

My father was the football coach at Coahoma Community College, and my mother worked in the cafeteria. I attended Bayou Elementary School, and then, because I lived on campus, I went to Coahoma Agricultural High School. I couldn't attend Clarksdale High School because it wasn't integrated, but I later finished at Coahoma Junior College, briefly attended Tupelo College, and eventually earned my bachelor's degree from Rust College. Later, I received my master's in education from Mississippi State University, and I got my certification in administration from Delta State University. When I graduated from Rust I just wanted to teach. I started in the high school, and I taught world history, American government, economics, and U.S. history. I can attest to the fact that there wasn't a day gone by when it was easy just to teach the classes, go home at 3:30, and come back the next day. I enjoyed teaching, and I can't remember ever planning on being an administrator.

I can't remember the first year I taught at an integrated school because even in high school we had one little white guy in our school. And there were always white teachers, but there weren't a lot of white students. By the time I started teaching in 1971 and 1972 integration had already occurred. When I worked at Coahoma Agricultural High School as a teacher, our basketball team won several state championships, but what was even more rewarding to me was when our smart, well-adjusted black children made the transition from Aggie to Ole Miss, or Mississippi State, and they did well as students. For them to successfully make that transition, then be able to go anywhere in the country, that was just wonderful! I've heard people say that both the white and black middle-class folks are leaving Clarksdale because of the poor quality of the public school system, but that just isn't true. We work hard every day destroying that myth.

The state ranks all the schools, level 1 through 4, with 4 being the best. We are now ranked at level 3 and working toward level 4. As far as I'm concerned, we're the best in everything, and if we aren't, we will keep striving to be the best until we achieve that goal. In order to be the best, we're willing to take it upon ourselves to uphold the standards set by the school board, as far as dress code, discipline, tardiness, teachers being on duty, and accountability for teacher performance. It's a hard goal to reach, because it's difficult to attract good, young, dedicated teachers because of the low pay, and because they have to live in the Delta.

"We are a level 3 school striving to be a level 4."

My mother is seventy-seven years old, she's lived here a long time, and even though she's gotten adjusted, she'll tell you even today that she doesn't like living in the Delta. I used to hear Mr. McLauren, one of my teachers, say the same thing. He was from south Mississippi, and he just couldn't get used to living in the Delta. It's a problem we've had for a long time, and it's one that is difficult to overcome, but we have other problems that are much more pressing.

Our biggest problem is lack of support from parents. I love all these children, and I'm firm with them, but in some instances I have to send them home and tell them not to come back until they bring their parents with them. Many times the parents won't even come to the school. It is very sad. We can institute all the programs we want about teen pregnancy and drugs and alcohol and abusive relationships, but at some point all of those programs have to be supported by parents in the home, and that's where we have problems. For various reasons, many of these kids run their own households. They are the parents, and no matter how hard they try, they can't fulfill a role they are not yet ready to perform. One little girl got pregnant when she was a freshman, and then she got pregnant again when she was a senior. She's having to stay home because there is no one but her who can take care of her babies. It is very sad.

But we've spent too much time talking about our challenges. I'd like to tell you about some of our successes. Our Technical Preparation Program was recently selected as the number 1 program in the state of Mississippi for the second year in a row. That's a state program that coordinates technology, vocational courses, and academic classes, so that we are all working from the same page for the benefit of the student.

Another area where we have been very successful is in our teacher mentoring and counseling program. It is not state-mandated, but it is something we came up with several years ago. Each teacher is responsible for keeping up with the permanent academic records of the students in their homeroom. That keeps the students from falling through the cracks because they didn't receive adequate counseling. Although the program has added a little to the teachers' workload, they don't mind because they see it working.

In the future, if we are to overcome our challenges and continue our successful programs, we've got to get more parents involved. And when I say involved, I mean on a positive note, not a negative one. That means having parents, teachers, administrators, and most importantly students coming together to visit before there is a problem, and when a problem does develop, we can work our way through it with a sense of trust.

Also, when we built the new high school, I hoped that it would draw a significant number of children back to public schools from the private academies. But that has not happened. Our enrollments stay about the same. But I have decided that it would be wonderful if we could coordinate with the academies, and we could send them eight or ten of our best students, and they could send

us eight or ten of theirs. Although it hasn't yet happened, I know it can be done. I was told that last year when Clarksdale was playing ball in the tournaments, some of the kids from Lee Academy sat in the stands and cheered for Clarksdale. And I was also told that when our kids are not playing, they go watch Lee Academy play. That's the kind of good, positive interaction I'm talking about, and I've often said if you leave the kids alone, they'll solve their own problems. I know that's true, because we're very special people here.

Olenza Self McBride

Johnnie Billington

Bluesman and MacArthur Fellow • Lambert

I was born in Quitman County and was raised up here at Lambert, and then in 1955 I moved up North. I moved back about twenty years later. I came back because I decided that things had made a terrific change, and I wanted to play the blues here at home. Problem was, there was nobody really playing the blues anymore, not around here, and I'd been playing the blues since I was a child. After I moved back home, I decided I needed to get people to listen to the blues. The children walking by my house on their way to school would listen when they'd hear me playing the guitar. They'd stop, and they'd say, "Oh Jesus! I'd like to play a guitar like that." I'd tell them come over here, and I'd try to teach them how to play it. After I got a few kids to come by the house, I had an idea. I thought, why don't I try to teach one child in each family to play the blues? Crime is on the rise. A young man got killed right here in town a few days ago; somebody robbed and killed him. My theory is that we've got to educate kids outside of school. And I thought, well, if I can get something going that would attract their attention after school, maybe I could talk to them about not doing all the bad things there are to do out there. You see, all those kids looked happy, and they looked forward to what I said. I'd tell them, "You know, there's a brighter way, there's a brighter side of life. There's a better future."

I'm trying to help train these young people up with the right ideals. I was sad when I visited the school in Jonesboro, Arkansas, where that boy went back and killed those kids. I was there a couple years before that happened, and I performed, and I talked to the kids, but I didn't work a program there. And I believe if you had somebody pick up the tab and pay for people to counsel those kids, every day, chances are you would never see things like that happen.

We got kids around here and in Clarksdale getting knives and guns. But on the weekends, I have a lot of kids come over here, and it's very exciting because I know if they're here, then they won't be out getting into trouble. There's nobody here but me and my daughter, and this house has eight rooms. Sometimes the kids will call me up and say, "Mr. Billington, can you come and get us?" Well, I got this big lawn where they can play, and they got someplace comfortable to sleep, and that gives me the opportunity to talk with them some more. They'll say, "This is really nice." And I say, "Well son, you know how you get this? You got to work. They're not going to give you this house, and they're not going to give you all of the land around it. You've got to work for it."

"The blues is a state of mind as much
as it is a kind of music."

I've carried my message all over the state, but it takes a lot of work, and a lot of money to travel all over and educate these kids, and I wasn't that financially able. The Mississippi Arts Agency gave me a little funding, and the private sector pitched in a few dollars here and there, and it looked really beneficial, but really, it didn't help the kids that much, because the money didn't go for the right resources. So me and the kids decided to make our own money. We'd hold concerts here in the backyard, and the kids would play, and we'd attract quite a crowd—150 or 200 people.

I bought this house just to help support the kids' concerts. It's in a perfect location. We're right on the highway, and the state won't allow anyone to park on the highway, so I fixed the stage in such a way that you can't see the concert unless you pull into my yard and pay to park. I put the band stand on the northeast side of the property, so that at 2 o'clock that big old tree would keep the whole band in the shade until 6 o'clock. That protected our entertainers from the sun, and it kept anybody from being able to see the band without pulling in here and paying for parking. Pretty soon we started drawing big crowds, and when everyone saw they would have to pay to see the performance, they did. This gave the boys some money for their work, and it also taught them something about business sense, about making money, and about how it was better to earn it than it was to try and take it off of someone else.

Sometimes they'd say, "How can I play the blues? I don't know how to read music?" And I'd tell them that most blues artists didn't read music. They got their ideas from nature and the things they heard around them. Like the birds chirping in the trees, back when there were trees, and people working in the fields, back when people worked in the fields. So they were listening to nature, and they was trying to get the guitar and keyboard to do what they heard in nature. Or sounds they heard in their day-to-day lives. They might hear the old train going through Lambert, moving real slow, going chugga-chugga, chugga-chugga, up the grade, and they'd try to make their guitar sound the same.

Then the train would speed up, and when it hit the cracks where the rails were joined together, and it would go clackity clack, clackity clack, clackity clack, and they'd speed up their playing to match that sound. Or they might be in the back of a truck going to the field or to town, and when the truck tires would hit the cracks between the concrete pads it would go clickety, clickety, clickety, and somebody in the truck would start singing a song to match that rhythm. If the truck got slower or faster somebody would hit the hood of the truck, they'd holler at the driver, "Hey, slow it down. You're messing up the rhythm of our song." The blues players couldn't read music, but they got their rhythms and timing right by using another technique. That's the technical end of the blues, but there is another side to it as well.

The blues is a state of mind as much as it is a kind of music. When the brothers and sisters created the music, they were singing and playing about things that happened in their everyday lives. Maybe your lady gave you problems last night, or maybe you had a little argument, or maybe your boss called you in and he treated you wrong; tomorrow you might be singing the same song, but you don't feel the same way. Tomorrow, you're going to put a little bit more emphasis on one part, and you'll take off some and add more somewhere else. It's about how your feeling, regardless of how you feel. That's why the blues is not a music that covers just one person; it covers everybody. You get up in the morning and you have a bad day today. You get up tomorrow and you want to do better. You get up with the idea that I'm going to work a little harder, and try to do better because I didn't do too good yesterday. So you're going to be feeling a little bit different, and you work a little bit harder. It's like that with a blues artist. He finds a scratch on your soul, and he just keeps digging, and digging and digging, until it gets to be a sore, and you can feel it; that's what the blues is all about—feeling.

Sister Teresa Shields

Director • Jonestown Learning Center • Jonestown

I represent the four Holy Name Sisters from the state of Washington. I came from Seattle to Jonestown in 1984. Two of us taught at Immaculate Conception Church School in Clarksdale, and two of our senior sisters taught in our home in the after-school program. They also held rummage sales, and they started the box project here, which is families helping families from the north to the south. In 1990, Immaculate Conception closed and for two years I taught at Saint Gabriel's down in Mound Bayou, but that closed in 1992, and I asked the community if we could start the Jonestown Learning Center. The community enthusiastically agreed, and then with a grant from the Phil Hardin Foundation, we got this beautiful building for a very fair price. It had been empty for a year and a half, and there were a lot of broken windows. It was even known as a crack house, but with a lot of help from a lot of Jonestown people, as well as people from around the country, we fixed it up, and one week after we got the key, the children, who are truly a blessing, started coming, and they've been coming ever since.

We have a licensed preschool which is a half-day preschool for two-, three-, and four-year-olds who don't go to Head Start in the morning. We have them from about three to three and a half hours in the morning. After they go home, we have a little break, and then about 2:45 in the afternoon, elementary students in grades K–5 come to the center, and we help them with their homework. We provide help in reading, math, computer classes, art activities, and language activities. Two evenings a week, we also have a Girls to Women class for girls in the fourth, fifth, and sixth grades, which concerns teen pregnancy and prevention class.

Once a week we also have a Little Big Brothers program for fourth-, fifth-, and sixth-grade boys. We talk to them about self-esteem, values, responsibility, honesty, avoiding drugs, alcohol, and life on the street. This past spring we were grateful to have a little grant so we could teach a parenting class called STEP, which Maxine teaches, and RETANCE. We had twenty graduates in that class, and one of them had perfect attendance. We have two AmeriCorps volunteers, who came to us in 1992 when President Clinton started the program.

Some people are amazed at how we staff the place, since our budget is practically nonexistent. I tell them we advertise in the paper, and we go to the local community colleges, and when we ask for volunteers locally, the cream

"We talk to them about self-esteem, values, responsibility, honesty, avoiding drugs, alcohol, and life on the street."

in Jonestown rises to the top. We've had some wonderful women working here, and some of them have gone on to not necessarily bigger and better things, but to other jobs in the community and in ministries. And sometimes they stay and help out here, because they want to spend their time and energy helping their kids and their own community. At all the workshops I attend, they are always talking about stakeholders. These women are mothers and grandmothers who are stakeholders in the Jonestown Learning Center. They are very concerned about getting an education for their children. That's certainly an impetus for people to get involved and stay involved and see that our initial success continues, rather than having people involved who are just here as a passing fling.

Little Dreamer
Our Lady of Lourdes
Elementary School
Greenville

Claire Drew

English Teacher • Clarksdale High School • Clarksdale

We moved to Clarksdale from Memphis in January 1970, when my father was hired as the editor of the *Farm Press*. We'd only been here a month when a federal court ordered the schools integrated. Integration created a lot of fear and confusion, but mostly people were worried because things had gotten pretty violent in other places. As I recall, their fears weren't justified, because from a teenage perspective, everything here seemed to go pretty well. Even so, in response to the court order, a lot of white parents formed an all-white academy, and that's where they sent their children. I was one of them; although I had started at Clarksdale High School, my parents moved me to Lee Academy. I didn't think much about it at the time, because as a student, I wasn't too concerned about social issues. Like most teenagers, I was more concerned about my friends, who I was dating, and other teenage problems. When I got to college things changed. I met people from many different cultures, and I was so glad that I did.

After I graduated from college, I started teaching in the public schools. It was as much a monetary decision as anything else. The state paid much better than the private school system. Back then my gross pay was $800 per month, and I think I took home a little over $500. But that was better than what the private school teachers were making. Now, even though my original decision was economic, I have become convinced that it is important for students to get to know people of all different cultures, the same way I did. I don't think any student, black, white, Asian, or whatever, needs to be isolated with members of their own race and culture. I understand that the academies have done some integrating, too, and I think that's admirable.

Not all my students feel that way. We don't have fights and that sort of thing, but I know that there are those who have prejudices against other culture groups, and they don't mind sharing their feelings. But there are other students who really appreciate diversity. Last week, when we were writing in our journals, one of my white students wrote in his journal how much he enjoyed the diversity at the school. He said it had given him an opportunity to see people from other races, different religions, and opposing points of view. I wasn't just pleased by his response; I was also pleased by how well he expressed himself, because that is my primary job.

I teach sophomore English, which includes literature, grammar, and writing. I try to teach my students the five-paragraph model. I tell them it is a recipe, like baking a cake. I tell them they can get fancy with the beautiful wedding

"I have become convinced that it is important for students to get to know people of all different cultures, the same way I did."

cakes later on, but they have to know the basics first. The state recently mandated a comprehensive writing test in order to graduate, and we just took it two weeks ago. They had to write a narrative and an informative essay. The highest score they can make is four, but two is passing, and to be honest, some of my kids are shooting for a two. But I'm proud of them. This is one of the weaknesses I see in the block schedule. They might not have had English for a year and a half, and even when they had it the first time, the teacher might not have stressed essay writing. I had to start from bare bones with some of them. But for the past nine weeks that's all we've done is write, write, write. Now we're getting ready to get into the literature book a little bit more, and that's where some of the fun stuff is located. But we still have to meet pretty rigid state standards.

Sometimes I wish we had more flexibility in the curriculum, but I must admit that I had gotten into a comfort zone with my teaching, and some of the new state standards have forced me to change my methods. I do think there needs to be something that lets all teachers know they will be held accountable, because it makes those who might not be doing their job perform at a higher level. These tests, however, should primarily be used as a diagnostic tool. If the students aren't performing well, then we need to look further back to the seventh, eighth, and ninth grade to see what preparation they've had before they took the test. So far the state seems to be changing and adjusting it to fit our needs, and that's good. I do see assessment as a positive thing, but I do resent having a test foremost in my mind all the time, hanging over everyone's head like the Sword of Damocles. Today, I had a student who came in and hugged me. When I first started working with him, he couldn't write a decent sentence. Today, he showed me his report card; he'd passed his test, and he'd gotten a B in English this term. That was very gratifying.

Clarksdale High School is a good high school. My son went to school here and I think he got an excellent education. We have a zero-tolerance drug policy, and we have several programs to deal with teen pregnancy, which not only is a problem here, but is a problem around the country. We have sociology classes to help students understand how to deal with other people, and psychology classes to help them understand themselves. We teach employability skills to help students get and keep a job. I personally take them out on tours to local businesses where the owners and managers tell them what kind of employees they want. During black history month, I have them write about people they admire from any culture, other than their own. I work with some fabulous teachers, and our principal is a very strong leader. She doesn't take any nonsense off of anyone. She does what's right even if it's not popular. She's not afraid to do that. We've won several state championships in athletics, and academically we are a level 3 school striving to be level 4. I love this community, the kids, and the school. I think God has blessed me because I have a job that I like, and when I wake up Monday morning I say, "Oh boy, I get to go to work!"

Cristen Craven Barnard

Artist • Tutwiler

When I was a little girl, my grandparents had a grocery store south of Clarksdale, and I sat on the front porch and listened to people play blues and gospel music. I think it just stuck in my head. Since I couldn't sing or play, I guess I just drew what was in my head. I've been painting as long as I can remember. I think my work really looks like the Delta; it's got the rich colors and the heritage of the Delta. I also do children's portraits, but I'm best known for my murals. I'm currently doing a historical timeline for the Delta Cultural Center in Helena, Arkansas. One side is 130 feet long, and the other side is 60 feet long; it actually turns the corner at one end. I had to do a lot of research for this project, particularly in the area of plants that were native to the region, and architecture. There's also a little bit about blues music, but it's mostly an overall history of the area: the Civil War battles, the animals that are native to the banks of the Mississippi River, and the Indian culture, particularly the mounds and dwellings where they lived.

I've grown up listening to stories that are wonderful. And they're not sad stories. They're always really funny, and, even when times were hard, there was something good, life-affirming, and positive in them. I guess my work is an outgrowth of the blues and gospel music that got stuck in my head, and the visual representation of the storytelling I heard. That's why I love the people in the Delta.

I see them as a proud people. With or without money they are proud. I'm aware that there are poor people here, but I don't exactly see the situation as one of poverty. To me, there's more poverty if I go to a big city and everybody is jam-packed in little apartment buildings, with no yards and no place to put out a garden. Here, the people may not have big homes, or even very nice homes, but they have a lot of freedom to come and go as they please any time—day or night—and everyone has a small garden beside his house.

After I graduated from the University of Southern Mississippi, my husband and I tried living in Jackson and Slidell and Baton Rouge, but when I got ready to raise a family, I wanted to raise my kids here. Their grandparents are here, and we see that as an important connection for our kids, and we know all the people here. We know that if our kids do something wrong someone will either call us, or they'll stop them right there and say, "Don't ride your bicycle out here. You'll get hit by a car." It doesn't bother us if somebody else gets onto our children, because we know a lot of people, and they know us.

*"I think my work really looks like the Delta; it's got
the rich colors and the heritage of the Delta."*

I'm always around kids, either mine or someone else's, particularly when I'm working on a mural. I've got a group of ten that I'm going to be working with this summer, and they've all had a good bit of high school art. They'll be turning in a portfolio where I can evaluate it and kind of work with them on their strengths and weaknesses, but what I really want them to realize is that they can survive doing art. They might have to paint signs, and they may have to do a lot of grunge work, but that enables them to do the fun stuff. And I want the kids to realize that, because there are lots of different things to do in the art field, like computer art or color separation.

I try to provide the same experience I had when I was thirteen or fourteen with two artists from Tupelo. I'm doing the same thing, and it meant a lot to me. I still run across one of the guys that I worked with; he's even judged competitions that I've been in. I feel like by working with these kids, and being a good role model, I'm teaching them how to be professional artists. That means meeting their deadlines and being on time for appointments and not giving excuses when they come up short, because people don't care for excuses, in the regular world or the art world, either. I try to teach them to go about their art like they would any other job, plus some.

Home of the Blues,
mural by Ron Brower

I'm not the only artist in the Delta. Marshall Bouldin is one of the top portrait artists in America. I don't run with Marshall Bouldin, but I know him, and I hope he knows my work. A lot of local artists show together, and a few times a year we'll put on a community arts program. Everybody helps everybody else if they hear about jobs, or grants, or shows, or things of that nature. And if someone approaches me with a job I can't do, then I'll usually refer them to someone else.

Tutwiler has several artists, like Leslie Turner, who does stained glass and pottery. She lives up towards Vance. Melanie Bruster does sculptures, and her son is also an artist. He does surrealistic paintings, and her father does a lot of leather work. The man two doors down makes beautiful furniture, and we also have another furniture maker here. I sell a lot of my prints in *Living Blues* magazine, and I also sell my work at crafts shows and galleries. They're building a huge gallery over in Helena, and they are building some shops over there as well. The Delta Cultural Center is helping revitalize the town in several stages. It's wonderful!

Part Four

WORKING THE LAND AND WATER: A PHOTO ESSAY

A Dying Breed • Mississippi River Steamboat

Junkyard Assembly Line • Greenwood

State of the Art • Delta Cotton Gin

"The worst one was in 1927, if the levee had held."

Flood Marks • U.S. Army Corps Of Engineers • Vicksburg

Levee Maintenance Road • Friars Point

Delta Sun • Anywhere in the Delta

Waiting for a Dry Spell • Pivot Irrigation Sprayer

Break!

Heading North • Clarksdale

Moving Freight on the Mississippi • Helena

Part Five

A DELTA DREAM

Sunday Best • Downtown Motor Inn • Clarksdale

Terry "Big T" Williams
Local Bluesman
Clarksdale

Boiled Blues (for the Mississippi Delta)

Nikki Giovanni

I like my blues boiled with a few tears
On the side
I like my men a little crazy
And my women to be good friends
I like my sons bold
And my daughters brave
I am the Mississippi delta

I like my people black

Nobody understands why they stayed with me
The folks who drained this basin were as mean
As a rattlesnake waking up at dawn

You do not have to take this
Seriously
If you take it seriously
You will sweat the magic
You will blind the magic
The magic will not sing

I want mud on my breasts
And honey on my toes
And something really great
Against my thighs

Come on Baby
Come on baby come on baby
Dance with me

Does a nudist wear an apron
When she cooks

I like my water on tap
My beans dried
And hot sauce on my chitterlings

If I were a shower
I could saturate your hair
Work my way over your lips
Across your shoulders
Around your waist
Through your knees
To the tips of your toes
And back again
Warm wet salty
Sweet

But I'm a River
Started because an ice field fell in love
With the sun
Started small
You can jump me
In Minnesota
But I ate well and grew

I am the Delta
I am black
And unafraid of the wind
I caress the Crescent City
I bring the blues

This time
I'll take mine fried

Present-Day Mansion
Highway 61 South

Growing Up in Indianola

Robin Rushing
Writer/Public Relations, Lyon

The White Citizens Council was formed in Indianola in a house across the street and down from my great-grandparent's home, the house where my oldest brother now lives. That particular organization was what could fundamentally be called the White Collar Ku Klux Klan, and the original White Citizens Council spawned others like it throughout the South and beyond. My great-grandfather was the city clerk of Indianola, and while he was not a wealthy man he did have a respected social standing in the community.

I can remember when I was little, my great-grandfather attended weekly meetings with other prominent men of the community. I was always told they were "playing dominos." I realize that subjects such as civil rights were not things that were generally talked about in my family back then, but if you apply a few critical thinking skills it's not too hard to figure out that those men weren't playing dominos. I'm sure if I went back and did the research, some of my family members would come up in the Sovereignty Commission papers somewhere— not that it would be anything to cheer about. I have no concrete proof, but it is only logical to assume that my great-grandfather belonged to the White Citizens Council during that time.

My family and I lived on Sunflower Avenue, directly across from both my maternal great-grandparents and grandparents. It was wonderful having such an immediate extended family, but for me growing up in the 1960s was just a weird time in general.

I remember the civil rights era in the Mississippi Delta as a time when it seemed like every kid experienced chaos and turmoil on some level. I don't care how pastoral the environment, we were all just going go through this upheaval— some of us with our hormones kicking in—and then with all the war and racial stuff added it was just a mess.

My great-grandfather died when I was about six years old, but my grandfather was still alive and I was real fortunate to have him around. Even though he was an alcoholic, I didn't care how much he drank because he was just a cool, cool man. He was a World War II navy veteran and amateur radio buff. He turned me on to international radio, where people were talking all over the world through ham. My father, who taught electronics at a local community college, was an amateur radio enthusiast as well. He was also a patented inventor who made extra money repairing radios and TVs and serving as a first class engineer for most of the local radio stations. As it turned out, I grew up with more exposure to the airwaves than most folks my age.

After being introduced to all this media, it's no wonder I found my salvation in my little tabletop Zenith AM radio. The cover was melted where someone had laid a hot soldering iron on top, which was neat because it allowed me to see the tubes glowing inside. It looked gimpy, but it worked. At night I could pick up WLS radio, right out of Chicago, and that quickly became my way of dealing with all the chaos around me. I latched onto music. I don't know any other way to say it: music was just my salvation. All the electronics I was introduced to by my grandfather and father broadened my view, and it helped me begin to understand that there was more going on in this world than just what was happening right there in Indianola, Mississippi.

Listening to WLS on any given night I could hear Aretha Franklin, Gary Lewis and the Playboys, James Brown, The 1910 Fruit Gum Company, The Animals—rhythm and blues, pop, and rock—all on the same station! It was an amalgamation of different styles and different influences because, obviously, radio stations back then weren't specialized like they are now. Like I said, I grabbed hold of music and I pretty much channeled my life into that area. It helped settle some of the inner and outer conflict I was feeling and gave me a more democratic view on life. My heroes came in all shapes, colors and sizes, mostly on 45 rpm, via the airwaves.

My other outlet was writing. I come from a long line of writers: my great-grandmother was a writer and journalist, my oldest brother is a newspaper editor, another brother is a gardening author, and I have an aunt who writes Christian literature. Even my "nonwriting" brother pens a mean poem. He once wrote the lines: "I'll do responsible in a minimum mode/to gain a maximum free." As a kid, I thought that was just revolutionary. Words—broadcast, spoken, and written—were just in my blood and part of my culture. Eventually, I started focusing most of my attention on writing and music, trying to cope with and/or escape the chaos around me. Like a lot of adolescents, I felt I didn't fit in. In this case, I really didn't.

I also come from a long line of what a lot of people in my hometown would call intellectual weirdoes. My oldest brother taught himself Greek at an early age. My middle brother was one of the first long hairs in Indianola, but he didn't smoke dope, and he sang in the church choir every Sunday. My other brother rejected the system outright and became sort of a brilliant loner working nights at the local truck stop and spending the rest of his time riding his European bicycle for miles out into the country. And, of course, Granddaddy, known for his tall tales, was one of two town drunks—Indianola was so small they had to take turns. While most kids had dogs or cats for pets, my family had a coatimundi

donated from an eccentric great aunt in New Orleans and a red fox salvaged from a den tilled up in a cotton field. I needed writing just to help me establish a little order.

A Good Time
Was Had by All!
Delta Blues Festival
Greenville

The things that I remember most vividly about growing up in the Delta are the people coming in from the fields on Saturday night. And how downtown Indianola rocked on those nights! We would get our allowances, Mom and Dad would take us downtown, and it was, like, "Look out Morgan & Lindsey and Ben Franklin!" The Honey Theater would be showing Elvis movies, and we felt "Yahoo, it's Saturday night!" Spend your allowance, one, maybe two dollars; taking hours to spend those dollars. And up and down the street there were just throngs of people who worked their asses off during the week. They were mostly sharecroppers and domestics and people like that, but downtown Indianola would rock 'til midnight on Saturday night!

Of course, you're hard-pressed to find a downtown these days in the Delta—a thriving downtown—and if you do find one it's usually closed up by five or six o'clock because people are afraid some unknown boogie man will get them. There are a few exceptions. But I still remember how it was back then, the mass of people, and I remember the old, blind white man in front of the Piggly-Wiggly playing the blues on an ancient, battered, blonde, double cut-away acoustic guitar with a tin cup duct-taped to the head stock. And I remember the hot tamale cart man, selling bundles of tamales wrapped in old issues of the *Commercial Appeal* to soak up some of the reddish grease. That's what I remember most, a thriving populace in my town when I was growing up. But I didn't know any of the black people, and except for those Saturday nights downtown I didn't really have anything to do with other races. I didn't have any opportunity to mix.

Now, having said that, my family did have black women who came into our homes and worked as what we called our maids—but they weren't really our maids. They were our caretakers. One in particular, Dora Clerk, was a real loving and strong presence for me growing up. She was about as big as a door; she was massive and could be the most frightening woman, but also the most loving. Basically, I needed someone like Dora in my life to reel in my butt, because I was a wild child. I'm still a wild child, much to many people's chagrin. But back then I mean I *was* wild! If I were a kid these days I'd be diagnosed with some condition or another and pumped full of pills and channeled into special classes. Back then I sort of ran amok, mainly in an effort to get noticed in my large and rather loose-knit family.

I'm the youngest of four kids, and I'm the only girl. My mother was married when she was fifteen and had my oldest brother a year later at sixteen. My dad was in the marine corps and served in the Korean War; he was a survivor of the Chosin Reservoir campaign. After leaving the military, he took a position as an advanced electronics professor at the local community college in Moorhead. As for my mother, after giving birth to three stair-step boys, I think she was pretty tired and otherwise perplexed when a baby girl came along in 1958. I was a difficult birth, a breech baby, and I don't think my mother and I ever really bonded. She used to say, "Robin Elizabeth Rushing, you came into the world butt first and you've been a butt ever since."

She was, for the most part, a homemaker but she did work at a few jobs outside the home. When I was in grade school she worked at the local welfare office and later on in a local pharmacy selling jewelry and cosmetics. I was sick a lot, and she had to work to help pay the medical bills. For whatever reason, my mom just couldn't handle me—but Dora sure could. She was literally and figuratively a looming, large presence early on in my life. Because of Dora I never felt I was without guidance or love.

So I grew up with this duality about race. I cherished my relationship with Dora, and I was familiar with two of her daughters, but I didn't really know any other black people. She was nevertheless a very important part of my life, and to this day I'm still trying to somehow resolve in my mind the connected but separate lives we shared. The duality became particularly troublesome for me when I was seven or eight years old, during Freedom Summer. I can remember when the civil rights movement took hold in Mississippi, and all of a sudden the little cafés in the Delta were turned into key clubs. The "key" was you had to be white to be served. There was this one tiny coffee shop, Dalton's, in downtown Indianola, and I vividly recall when they turned it into a key club. People would come in and sit at the counters, sure, but they were all white and had been given a "complimentary" key, or maybe they paid a dollar for it, I don't know for sure. All that I really cared about at that time was an ice-cold Orange Crush in a brown bottle served with an icy café waterglass on the side.

When I think back to that and other summers I also think about being outside in our large yard and playing along Indian Bayou. Our property line ran out into the bayou, and when I was a kid I had this whole wonderful southern scenario at my disposal. I was given free rein to run up and down that bayou; my mom's loud, two-fingered wolf whistle was the signal to get home, and we knew how far we could stray and still be within whistling distance.

But one day when I was playing on the edge of the sluggish, brown water some Freedom Marchers came to Indianola, walking down Main Street. Our properties were on either side of Sunflower Avenue with Indian Bayou running parallel between our houses and Main Street. When the Freedom Marchers walked through town, the white citizens were suddenly out in their yards and on the streets—offended—saying "Look at those people, how dare they!" They took out their little cameras, so they could take pictures that would identify the rabble-rousers to "authorities" later on.

Now I was only about seven or eight years old when that happened, but looking back on my life I think that seeing those Freedom Marchers was the beginning of a political awakening for me. Because even at that young age, I could tell that "those people" were just walking down Main Street. They weren't rabble-rousing, they weren't rioting, they weren't making any kind of gestures toward us, or yelling back at us. They were just walking down the street. I think that was the first time I had looked at the people around me and thought how ridiculous we all appeared.

Another incident that still weighs heavy on my memory is when they desegregated the schools. I was in the sixth grade at Lockard Elementary School when it happened. Lockard was a public school, but it was an all-white public school. There had been a couple of brave black parents who put their children into Lockard, but it didn't last long. At the time black and white schools in Indianola were completely separate, even though they were public. I had rheumatic fever in the fourth and fifth grades, and I didn't go to school much for a couple of years. I was home-schooled even though that's not what we called it at the time. I spent a lot of time in bed battling my illness. I also spent a lot of time with my drunk grandfather; we sort of co-babysat each other. Dora was always nearby, too. By the time sixth grade rolled around, though, I was just getting my feet wet again in school. Then at mid-semester, the next thing I know, I'm going to school in the First Baptist Church in Indianola. I didn't understand, but I knew that it had to do with desegregation, and I also knew that in my house it wasn't a subject that was open for discussion. To me, insult was added to injury: I wasn't even Baptist!

The Indianola Academy had been formed a couple of years before the schools were ordered desegregated, but I was an unwilling recruit. The school's enrollment was predominantly planters' children and the richer kids who lived in town. My dad was a teacher, so we weren't rich by any means. We owned our house, we were adequately clothed, we had plenty to eat, and we owned one car. We had everything that we needed and then some, but we certainly didn't belong to the country club. We were secure, but most of the kids at the academy were rich kids—and I wasn't one of them. When told that I would be attending the academy I remember asking, "Why do I have to do this?"

But my dad, the ex-marine, didn't want to hear any whining. The second semester of my sixth-grade year was one of complete turmoil; each week I had to bring my school supplies in on Monday and take everything home on Friday because the church had Sunday School classes in our rooms. So I had to lug all my books, pencils, and notebooks back and forth between the church and my home the entire semester. The following year I attended classes at the academy proper: a series of metal pre-fabricated buildings in what was formerly a cotton field on the outskirts of town.

The longer I went to the academy, the more I realized it was all about race and desegregation. I remember pleading with my parents, "Why can't I go to the public school? These people are just racists." I also remember my dad telling me, "You don't need to know why we're sending you there, and it's not your decision anyway. We're your parents and it's our decision." Eventually I realized that, at least for my parents, it wasn't really about race. "It's about your education! It's about your education!" my father eventually said, emphatically, over and over in answer to my complaints. It wasn't until I got much older that I understood what he was talking about. Later on I understood that with desegregation most of the experienced, white teachers from the predominantly white public schools had gone into the private school system. And since the public school system had to be completely restaffed and revamped, things sank into even more chaos. For about ten years they just struggled to bring people in to the Mississippi Delta to fill the public school positions, and the people they brought in may or may not have had teaching experience. It was like they just needed a warm body up there in front of the kids. This happened in the academy school system as well, but to a much lesser extent.

Regardless of the reason I was enrolled in the academy, I did get an excellent education, and some of the teachers made a lifelong impression on me. In hindsight, I honestly believe for my family it was about education, not race. My dad was an educator; he wanted me to go where the best teachers were, and at

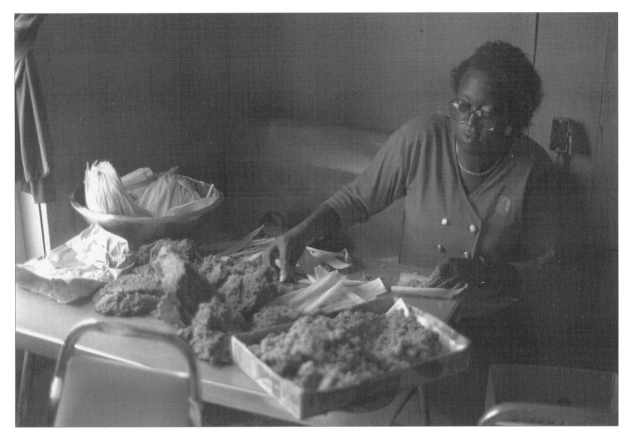

Delta Tamales
Old Country Store
Rosedale

that time the best teachers were in the private school system. They were the educators that he knew, valued, and trusted. I'm sure there were experienced and capable teachers in the public schools during that time, but the bureaucracy involved with school desegregation simply overwhelmed the system; or, at least it appeared that way to my father, and, over the years, I've become inclined to agree.

Through everything that has happened to me, and everything that I have experienced in my life, there has always been this burning desire to try to articulate why I feel somehow different. I keep trying to explain to myself and others how my upbringing and experiences in the 1960s Mississippi Delta color my take on the world. It's just a compelling desire to get to the bottom of the conflict and this need to express what the Delta means to me, for good or for ill. As an adult student at Millsaps College in the 1990s, I was taught by people like Shelby Foote, Paul Gaston, and C. Vann Woodward. At that time Woodward was professor emeritus of history at Yale. His book *The Burden of Southern History* was featured as a text in the college centennial's Eudora Welty Chair of Southern Studies course "Mythology and the South." Woodward was the first person that articulated—or even came close to articulating—why, as a southerner, I felt different.

His whole premise was that the reason we feel different in the South is because we *are* different. The American ideal doesn't apply to us in the Deep South; it has never applied to us. Southern history is not American history. In the South we didn't win all of our wars—even before Korea and Vietnam. The South's not always a land of plenty by any means. The South was certainly not a place where under the law people were created equal and given equal opportunity. The Mississippi Delta, of course, has been called the most Southern place on earth by historian James C. Cobb. When I read his book by the same name, I thought to myself, "Well, I guess he's right!"

Yet, as part of America, most of us in Mississippi Delta have done an amazing job of recovering from and repairing the chasms that existed before I was born and widened for a while as I grew up. Since the 1960s I have done my part; I have struggled within and without on issues of race and equality. I have learned hard lessons many times via the hard way. But through it all I have felt a sense of togetherness, of dependency on one another, regardless of race or economics. I feel my generation was pivotal, and I'm proud to have played a miniscule part in some of that change . . . even if it's only change within myself. Today I don't have to categorize my friends and colleagues in terms of "blacks" or "whites." To my way of thinking, we are pretty much in this together.

Like the rest of America, the Delta still has its share of ignorant jerks of all colors; I can be one of them. But there are many, many more good, caring and open-minded people; I can be one of them, too. But just like my relationship with Dora, that duality of life in the Delta has made me a richer, better person—even as I struggle to make sense of it all.

Nothing Can Change a Made-Up Mind!

David Jordan
State Senator, Twenty-fourth District, Greenwood

I believe that the Mississippi Delta can become an oasis, but for that to happen we must first start with education. Education is essential to the future of this region, just like it is anywhere else. When I was growing up, most of the people who worked and harvested the crops in the Mississippi Delta were African Americans. My parents and grandparents were sharecroppers and they never had an opportunity to attend school. I only had limited opportunities; during my grade-school days, I only attended classes four or five months a year, depending on the size of the crop we made. That created problems for me because when I entered the Greenwood Public School System, I failed, due to all those short years in grade school. But nothing can beat a made-up mind, and after a great deal of work, I graduated from Broad Street High School in 1955. After graduation, a lot of my classmates immediately left Greenwood, but me, I didn't have the bus fare to get out of town, let alone tuition for college. So I took a dishwasher's job at the Holiday Inn, the first one in town. I started out washing dishes, eventually became the salad boy, and finally worked myself all the way up to evening cook. That provided enough money for me to go to school. During the day I went to Mississippi State Valley College, and I worked the evening shift at the Holiday Inn. In 1959 I was the first person in my family to graduate from college, with a degree in science. I also had a trade!

At that time, I thought graduate school was out of the question, but when the Russians launched Sputnik, America was in the space race, whether it wanted to be or not. I applied for admission to Ole Miss. I was turned down, because African Americans were not allowed to go to white schools. But I didn't let that stop me. After being turned down, I applied to several universities out west, and I won a scholarship to the University of Wyoming. I went to graduate school in Wyoming three consecutive summers. When I was finished, I had a master's degree in science and was hired as a science teacher here at home. It's fair to say that the Russians and Sputnik had a great deal to do with me getting my degree. Since then I have attended Kansas State College, the University of Texas, Dillard University, and Tuskegee Institute. After attending several colleges and earning two degrees, I find that many children today don't appreciate all the hard work that it took for me to get where I am today. They want everything instant—right now!

"He spoke from his heart. That's why people listened to Martin Luther King Jr. And to Fannie Lou Hamer, Emmett Till's mother, and Rosa Parks, and all of the other nameless sharecroppers on unknown farms all over the Mississippi Delta and the South."

Children have no historic context in which to place themselves. That's partly because the church's presence has been diminished to some degree, and partly because history isn't taught in the schools. Since they don't know how they got where they are, children don't really understand or appreciate it. Children today need to learn that many people died changing the system. My dad died. He was just an illiterate man, with no education, but because of his drive and his will-power, he ended up being recorded on a record that is now in the Smithsonian. He was no great scholar, and he had no formal training, like I was fortunate enough to have. He just spoke from his heart. That's why people listened to Martin Luther King Jr., and to Fannie Lou Hamer, Emmett Till's mother, and Rosa Parks, and all of the other nameless sharecroppers on unknown farms all over the Mississippi Delta and the South. Conditions changed because people listened, and they listened because people told it from the heart. It was tough, because they weren't just trying to change a social system—they were trying to change a mindset of an entire people.

A mindset is what controls a person—good or bad. For instance, if you take a lion or an elephant out of the jungle, and you put a big chain around his neck, it will raise Cain and rare up for a long time. Eventually though, it'll realize that it can't get out of the chain. Then you can take a little rope and put it around his neck and he'll never try to get loose. It's that same psychological rope that's been on African Americans, generation after generation, that was only recently removed but it is still weighing some of them down. It's the feeling of being a nobody, of nothing going for me, or I'm not going anywhere, so why should I try, because I'm black, and it's rougher for me than anyone else. Besides that, there's a strike against me no matter where I turn.

In my generation, about eight of us said to hell with that kind of mindset. So we made it! And we've been telling our stories ever since, even though the children today don't want to listen. They seem to think that we had a lot of money, and that's how we made it. The truth is, we didn't have a change of clothes. The reason we made it was because we had a made-up mind. And nothing is stronger than a made-up mind!

I was heavily involved in the civil rights struggle early on. It was tough. I had an opportunity to attend the Emmett Till trial as a freshman in college. Till was killed in Money, Mississippi, a town ten miles north of Greenwood. The killers were eventually acquitted by an all-white jury. It was one of the most heinous crimes! I have been in four documentaries about the crime, but over the years there have been so many stories told about it that it's hard to get all the facts straight. Efforts have been made to secure the store where Till allegedly whistled at a white woman in order to renovate it and turn it into a shrine in his honor. In fact, I've had people come here from Kansas, and they worked here and made contributions so that one day we could have a marker for him on the courthouse lawn in Greenwood.

Even though that's one thing I really want to do, we haven't gotten to that point as yet. Last year, however, I was fortunate enough to have Hwy 49N, from Greenwood to Tutwiler, Mississippi, named after Emmett. Last Saturday, somebody wrote KKK on the sign, but the highway department has already put up a new one, and they'll keep doing that until the vandalism stops. Today, we have more power because a lot of things have changed since the old days, as a result of our victories at the ballot box and in federal courthouses. But there are some things we still can't control—like education.

Even if we had a complete metamorphosis in the education system, we would still have a long way to go. When integration came the whites left—they abandoned the public schools. And when they abandoned the schools they said that they were leaving because the schools were not up to par, that the schools were not producing what they should produce. Well, they produced Morgan Freeman! They produced me! They produced doctors, lawyers, teachers, and many other people with careers. That was even before we had good books and good facilities. When I was growing up we didn't even have books unless they had four names in them already, and all the old buildings were falling down. Now the kids get new books, new buildings, and new everything. So the idea, the perception, that schools run by African Americans are not good schools is just simply not true. What they are really afraid of is that we are after retaliation because of the way we were treated. Nobody is after retaliation for what has happened to African Americans in the Mississippi Delta—certainly not me. We are not about that; we want to show them how government is supposed to work, for everyone, to treat everybody right!

L. H. Threadgill
Elementary School
Greenwood

We've been here three, almost four hundred years together, and if we will work together we can make it! We were not treated right, but that does not mean that we are not now going to treat whites right. So white people need to come on back to the public schools and build together with blacks. So far there is no move toward doing this, and it hurts us when we are trying to recruit industries to the area. When we get industry in here, some whites lure industry off into the private schools for their children, even though they want them to go to public schools. They don't want to pay for their children to go to private school, but we don't get any encouragement or cooperation from the white community. So the manufacturers who come here have to pay to send their children to private school. It's a real shame.

We have some big, new public schools, good schools sitting out here, level 3 and level 4, like Greenwood High School. Schools that are running well. Of course they have a few problems. What school doesn't? So some whites pretend there is something wrong with them, but the bottom line is that they don't feel like they should have to go to school with African Americans. For them, it's a way of life—their kid goes to private school because they went to private school, and it continues, each generation following the next. But it doesn't have to be that way.

Just look at me! When I came off the plantation we were cussed and threatened just for trying to go to school, and now, fifty years later, I am in the state senate, on the agriculture committee, making laws for everyone. And I'm also on the city council here in Greenwood. Who would have dreamed of that when we were sitting in that hot courthouse in Sumner, Mississippi, during the Emmett Till trial? One lesson I have learned in life is that you have to be very careful how you treat people on the way up, because they may still be there on the way down. The Bible's right; you reap what you sew, but that's not our intention. Nobody is after anybody, not from my perspective.

I'm looked upon as being a radical, because I sued everybody I had to sue in order to facilitate change and to secure my rights. When I got involved in civil rights issues, I was fired as a teacher, so I sued the school system until I got my job back. Then I sued the city of Greenwood to change the form of city government, and I won. So now we have a more representative form of government. I sued the state of Mississippi to change the congressional district lines so that African Americans could be elected to Congress. We won that fight! All of this was all done in federal court, and we used the legal system to help change things. Changing things has been hard work, but it's not like standing out in that hot afternoon sun, chopping cotton from one end of that long row to the other. That's where the blues got started.

The blues is a kind of strange music that comes out of hardship, and it not only expressed but actually depicted one's feelings. When someone picks cotton all day, and the boss man is giving him hell, cursing him, and calling him the N word, then he comes home, and the wife's caught the Greyhound Bus and gone, he ain't got nothing left *but* the blues. So you have to express that in some kind of way. The language may not have been adequate, with verbal mistakes and poor diction, but it was an expression of pure human misery. Here was a man crying out in distress because of the hardships that life had heaped upon him, and he came out with the blues. And now that strange sound that he made, that came out of pain, hardship, and desperation, is a strange kind of music that the world loves. But never forget that it came from the hardship people faced living and working in the Mississippi Delta.

A few years ago I discovered that B. B. King, who had been to thirteen kingdoms all over the world playing music for kings and queens, had never been invited to play at the state capitol of Mississippi. That is in indication of how highly regarded the accomplishments of African Americans were around the world but not within the state. I asked him if he would come if I had a B. B. King day, and he said he would. So, I drafted a bill that honored him on February 15, 2005. The governor came over to the senate, and the lieutenant governor of Arkansas came. We had a whole day dedicated to B. B. King and his music. During the ceremony B. B. cried like a baby. He said he had never had anything like that happen to him. The senate had never had that many people in it before. We had a glorious day! We can have more glorious days for Mississippi and the Mississippi Delta, but we won't have them until we start working together! Hopefully, that's starting to happen. This year, blacks and whites coauthored a bill to have civil rights taught in all the public schools in Mississippi. The senate approved it unanimously. Things like the B. B. King Day and the Civil Rights Bill give me hope that there is a new day coming!

Courtesy of Mississippi Department of Transportation

End of the Line
Train Barn
Greenville

Patti Carr Black, friend and traveling companion of the late Eudora Welty, is also the former head of the Old Capitol Museum of Mississippi History, a lifelong resident of Jackson, Mississippi, a noted Civil War historian, and a prolific writer. She has written or edited thirteen nonfiction books, including *Mules in Mississippi, Art in Mississippi: 1720–1980, The Southern Writers Quiz Book* and *The Natchez Trace.*

Jean-Philippe Cyprès Jean-Philippe Cyprès is an award-winning photographer originally from Paris, France, where he studied with internationally known photographer Cees De Hand. He has been living in Knoxville, Tennessee, for over twenty years, where he maintains a studio that produces portraits for actors, models, and performers. His work has appeared in *Vogue Paris, Rolling Stone Paris* and numerous magazine publications in the U. S. A. His striking images in both *Women and Coal* and this book not only capture his subjects' pain and struggle, but their dignity as well. He has produced photo-essays in France, Holland, Greece, the Ivory Coast, and Thailand.

Morgan Freeman is a well-known Academy Award–winning actor, originally from Greenville, Mississippi. He has many successful films to his credit, including *Driving Miss Daisy, Glory, The Shawshank Redemption,* and others too numerous to mention. Between making movies and flying all over the world for personal appearances, when Mr. Freeman is at home in the Delta, he helps manage two businesses: the blues club Ground Zero and the five-star gourmet restaurant Madidi. In his spare time, he enjoys working his horses, playing with his grandchildren, and helping with local projects.

Nikki Giovanni was born in Knoxville, Tennessee, and even though she grew up in Cincinnati, Ohio, she and her sister returned to Knoxville each summer to visit their grandparents. Giovanni graduated with honors in history from Fisk University. Giovanni is a world-renowned poet, writer, commentator, activist, educator, and publisher who has authored thirteen books of poems. Giovanni's book *Black Feeling, Black Talk, Black Judgment* brought her national attention. Her most recent poetry collection, *Acolytes,* appeared in 2007. Since 1987, she has been a University Distinguished Professor at Virginia Tech. The NAACP made her its Image Award Winner for Literature in 1998, 2000, and

2003, and she has also been named Woman of the Year by *Ebony*, *Ladies Home Journal*, and *Mademoiselle*.

Senator David Jordan says even as a young man he was deeply concerned by segregation and figuring out ways to help overcome the repressive social system in the Delta. He often spent his days thinking about questions he simply couldn't answer. Eventually, after working his way through college and becoming a school teacher, Jordan's efforts paid off. He was a founding member of the Greenwood Voters League, a group Jordan describes as a "rag-tag, grassroots organization and one maladjusted teacher." Through a series of lawsuits Jordan filed, he made it possible for black candidates to be elected to the Greenwood City Council, and he helped create the Second Congressional District, a seat now held by U.S. Rep. Bennie Thompson. In 1983 Jordan was elected to the Greenwood City Council, and in 1993 he was elected to the Mississippi State Senate. Since being elected, Jordan has worked tirelessly to enact legislation to help address civil rights issues yet to be overcome, while looking toward a better tomorrow for all Mississippians. No doubt this is why his efforts have been rewarded with recognition from civil rights leaders, humanitarians, and Presidents Jimmy Carter, Ronald Reagan, George Herbert Walker Bush, and Bill Clinton.

Randall Norris is the former development director of Haley Heritage Square, a cultural complex designed to honor Alex Haley, the Pulitzer Prize–winning author of *Roots.* He's also the founder of the Appalachian Writers Center, an award-winning fiction writer, a humanities presenter, and an author. In 1990, he was the project director for the exhibit that inspired *Highway 61: Heart of the Delta.* In 1998, he was coeditor of *Women of Coal,* a photo essay book featuring fifty-four women from the central Appalachian coalfields. Later that year, he was awarded a Ph.D. in American Culture Studies at Bowling Green State University. In 2001, he was named an Illinois Road Scholar, and the following year he was placed on the Fulbright Senior Specialist Program Roster. He is currently a professor of English and American Culture Studies at Sauk Valley Community College in Dixon, Illinois.

Robin Rushing was born in Indianola, Mississippi, and, as a child, was educated in both public and private schools. Her roots are sunk deep in the Delta. Rushing graduated from Millsaps College, where she had an opportunity to study with Shelby Foote and C. Vann Woodward. From them she says, "I learned that the American Dream doesn't necessarily hold true for us; we have not won all our wars, everyone is not created equal, and not everyone begins life with an equal opportunity." Her writing, particularly regarding the blues and contemporary musicians, is well known throughout Mississippi.

Christine Wilson is director of publications for the Mississippi Department of Archives. She is also the Managing Editor of the *Journal of Mississippi History,* an illustrated quarterly magazine with stimulating articles by distinguished scholars on the history of Mississippi, the Lower Mississippi Valley, and the South. In 2000 she edited a very popular book, *All Shook Up: Mississippi Roots of American Popular Music.* This book was the companion to a 1990 exhibit of the same name, held at the State Historical Museum in Jackson, Mississippi. Her essay in this book connects the state's blues legends to different cities, counties, and plantations found throughout the Delta.

Abbott, Dorothy, ed. *Mississippi Writers: Reflections of Childhood and Youth.* 4 vols. Jackson: Univ. Press of Mississippi, 1985–1991.

Barnwell, Marion, ed. *A Place Called Mississippi: Collected Narratives.* Jackson: Univ. Press of Mississippi, 1997.

Barry, John M. *Rising Tide: The Great Mississippi Flood of 1927 and How it Changed America.* New York: Simon and Schuster, 1997.

Bercaw, Nancy. *Gendered Freedoms: Race, Rights, and the Politics of Household in the Delta, 1861–1875.* Gainesville: Univ. Press of Florida, 2003.

Biles, Roger. *Memphis in The Great Depression.* Knoxville: Univ. of Tennessee Press, 1966.

Burns, Ken. *The Civil War,* selections. VHS. Walpole, NH: Florentine Films, 1990.

Clay, Maude Schuyler. With an Introduction by Lewis Nordan. *Delta Land.* Jackson: Univ. Press of Mississippi, 1999.

Cobb, James C. *The Most Southern Place on Earth: The Mississippi Delta and the Roots of Regional Identity.* New York: Oxford Univ. Press, 1994.

Cook, Bruce. Listen to the Blues. New York: Scribner's Sons, 1973.

Daniel, Pete. *Deep'n As It Come: The 1927 Mississippi River Flood.* New York: Oxford Univ. Press, 1977.

Evans, David. *Big Road Blues: Tradition and Creativity in Folk Blues.* Berkeley: Univ. of California Press, 1982.

Foote, Shelby. *The Civil War—A Narrative.* New York: Random House, 1958.

Grossman, Stefan. *Delta Blues Guitar.* New York: Oak Publications, 1969.

Hall, B. C., and C. T. Wood. *Big Muddy: Down the Mississippi Through America's Heartland.* New York: Dutton, 1992.

Henry, Aaron, with Constance Curry. *The Fire Ever Burning.* Jackson: Univ. Press of Mississippi, 2000.

Hightower, Sherrie, and Cathie Stanga, *Mississippi Observed.* Jackson: Univ. Press of Mississippi, 1994.

Kennedy, Frances H., ed. *The Civil War Battlefield Guide.* Second edition. Boston: Houghton Mifflin, 1998.

King, Anne R. *Walls of Light: The Murals of Walter Anderson.* Jackson: Univ. Press of Mississippi/Walter Anderson Museum of Art, 1999.

Light, Ken. With a Foreword by Robert Moses. *Delta Time: Mississippi Photographs.* Washington, D.C.: Smithsonian Institution Press, 1995.

Palmer, Robert. *Deep Blues: A Musical and Cultural History of the Mississippi Delta.* New York: Penguin Books, 1982.

Rankin, Tom. *Sacred Space: Photographs from the Mississippi Delta.* Jackson: Univ. Press of Mississippi, 1993.

Samuel, Ray, Leonard Huber, and Warren C. Ogden. *Tales of the Mississippi.* New York: Hastings House Publishers, 1955.

Sugg, Redding S., Jr. ed. *The Horn Island Logs of Walter Inglis Anderson.* Memphis: Memphis State Univ. Press, 1973.

Willis, John C. *Forgotten Time: The Yazoo-Mississippi Delta after the Civil War.* Charlottesville: Univ. of Virginia Press, 2000).

Woodruff, Nan Elizabeth. *American Congo, American Congo: The African American Freedom Struggle in the Delta.* Cambridge, Mass.: Harvard Univ. Press, 2003.

Index